The Texas City Disaster 1947

A Survivor's Story

Dr. W. Michael McCrocklin

Copyright © 2017 W. Michael McCrocklin

All rights reserved. No part of this book may be used or reproduced by. any means, graphic electronic, or mechanical, including photocopying, recording, taping or by any information storage retrieval system without the written permission of the author except in the case of brief quotations embodied in critical articles and reviews.

This book is for sale at amazon.com and www.armchairtheology.org

Because of the dynamic nature of the Internet, any web addresses or links contained in this book may have changed since publication and may no longer be valid. The views expressed in this book are solely those of the author and do not necessarily reflect the views of the publisher, and the publisher hereby disclaims any responsibility for them.

Cover image by Nicole Roberts

Edited by Timothy Mulder, Melissa Roberts, and Jeannie McCrocklin.

ISBN: 979-8-9989882-0-2 (p)
979-8-9989882-2-6 (hc)
979-8-9989882-1-9 (e)

Library of Congress Control Number 2025910414

Revision date: 05/28/2025

Dedication

This historically based story is dedicated to the memory of the brave men and women, who fought the fires, rescued and recovered their friends and neighbors, and rebuilt Texas City with very minimal governmental or other outside help.

Theirs is a story of true American grit and determination. For many of them, all members of Dan Rather's "Greatest Generation", the Texas City Disaster was more traumatic than World War II. They deserve any accolades they receive.

The American Red Cross performed in their usual commendable way and this dedication extends to their workers as well as firemen from all over the USA who responded.

Local clergy were among the heroes and their work should be explored by some historian.

C.T. (Tommy) McCrocklin and W. H. (Sandy) Sandberg were certainly not the only local heroes. Everyone in Texas City and La Marque gave up much; and only a few sacrificed little.

Table of Contents

La Marque 3

Texas City 5

Republic Oil 9

Prelude 15

Orange Smoke 25

Fire 35

The Gates of Hell 41

Texas City Schools 61

SS High Flyer 71

The Day After 77

The Gymnasium-Morgue 79

Federal Court 91

Flashbacks 95

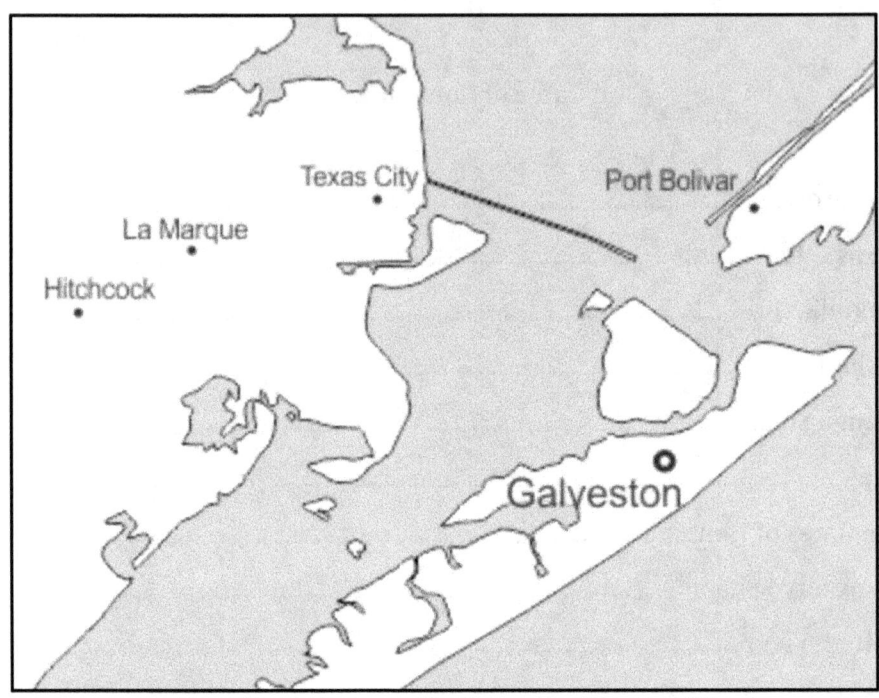
Texas City sits just over 40 miles south of Houston, TX.

1

La Marque
Summer, 1957

IT WAS ALREADY HOT, AND the humidity was 85 percent. Mike was mowing the front yard at 7:00 am, to avoid the 100-degree heat expected by noon. The lush Saint Augustine grass made it hard to push the rotary mower and he was already sweating profusely.

He looked up and saw an ominous looking black car with whip-like radio antennas turn into the crushed oyster shell driveway. He stopped the mower and stared. Mike was immediately afraid, and that fear grew when the man who got out of it was dressed as some kind of policeman, but not a local officer.

The lawman approached him and said, "Hi son. Is this the home of C.T. McCrocklin? Don't be scared. I have come to give him a ride to Federal Court in Houston. He knows someone is coming to give him a ride and escort him to court. Would you ask if he is ready to leave?"

At that moment, Mike's Dad came out the front door and said, "I am ready to go if you are, sir. Would you like a cup of coffee for the trip?" The marshal answered, "Yes, please. Black coffee is fine." C.T. went inside as the marshal turned and spoke to Mike again, "I guess it is not normal to see your dad put in a police car, is it?"

C.T. McCrocklin

No policeman had ever come to their home before, and Mike did not know what to think. He was still afraid and even though he was 14 years old he could not help the way his hands were shaking. He gulped, looking at the marshal and his powerful police cruiser. He had many questions but could not express even one of them.

Just then, C.T. came back with two cups and a thermos. The coffee was steaming, and its rich, dark aroma filled the sweltering air of the driveway, mingling with the smell of fresh-cut grass. Of course, the coffee smelled glorious, but Mike didn't understand why people drank that bitter stuff.

The marshal opened the front passenger door of the cruiser to allow C.T. into the front seat. The muffled roar of the big V8 engine made Mike long to go along for the ride. Somehow, he knew not to even ask if he could go to Houston, too.

As the car pulled away, Mike turned and ran in the house for a cold drink. He needed to calm his nerves. A cold Dr. Pepper would do just fine… A local Texas drink.

It was not until 7:00 p.m. when the marshal brought his dad home. Immediately after a later-than-normal supper of homemade hamburgers, the inquisitive teenager cornered his dad in the large living room and nervously asked, "Dad, are you in trouble?"

C.T. smiled and laughed. His blue eyes twinkled with humor. "No. Not at all. I was giving testimony in federal court. I am not in any trouble. I know you remember the Texas City disaster that killed over 600 people. The dead people have not all even been identified, even after ten years."

C.T. took a deep breath, his eyes lost in time. "Do you remember that I was the last man to leave the scene just before that first explosion? They cannot find anyone that was there just before the explosion, except me. Everyone else was killed."

C.T. looked at Mike and smiled softly. "The Court wants to know exactly who I saw at the pier and in the parking lots. There are a lot of people still missing, and they are trying to find out where they were just before the blast."

The tension left Mike immediately. "Oh. Good! I was afraid you were in trouble or something."

He did remember it well. In fact, he remembered nothing in his life before those horrendous days. The huge initial explosion was the first thing permanently recorded in his memory. As far as Mike's memory was concerned, life, for him, began shortly after 9:00 a.m. on April 16, 1947. It had been ten years, but the horror of those days came back to him as his Dad talked.

Another laugh came out, as C.T. sat down on the living room couch. He spoke over the buzzing sound of a Vornado fan sitting on the floor five feet away from them. "Well, the only trouble I will have is going to be remembering that horrible day and giving two or more weeks of testimony. With over 600 people killed, and as many as 180 of them unidentified, it is going to tax my memory quite a bit."

"I have not wanted to talk about it much, and since you were only four years old when it happened, I have not felt you needed to hear about it. I guess you are old enough now to hear more of the story. It was the worst industrial disaster in American history. It is a terrible story. I lost many friends and neighbors. Some of their bodies were never found." He said with a heavy sigh.

The Vornado buzzed on as C.T. told the story. Mike remembered some of it; but much of the information was new and fascinating…

2

Texas City

APRIL IS A SPECIAL TIME in southeast Texas. It is usually cool and often the normally high humidity drops to 30-to-40 percent. Tuesday, April 16, 1947, was a very beautiful day on the mainland in Galveston County.

The sky was light blue without a cloud in sight. The forecast was for clear skies, with high temperatures in the low 70's and light winds. Everyone in town knew that this was a respite before the brutally high summer humidity and scorching temperatures took over in mid-to-late May. By June 1, the daily highs could be near 100 degrees. Many of the women took advantage of the dry, sunny day to get wash loads done. Preschool children played in the tiny yards of the single-family wood-frame houses that made up most of the city.

Texas City has always been an industrial town, that is, it was designed to be a petrochemical powerhouse. Its small port is sheltered from the open Gulf of Mexico by Galveston Island. A five-mile-long earthen dike that was built into Galveston Bay, shielded on both sides by granite riprap. It acts as the longest man-made fishing pier in the world.

View from the Texas City dike. Used by permission from Melissa Roberts.

The riprap was made up of a combination of small and huge granite cubes; with the larger blocks often as much as ten feet on each side. That dike still provides very calm waters for all ships that dock at Texas City to this day. Its ownership was ceded by the state in the 1930's to the city of Texas City by the Texas legislature, only one week after its construction was finished.

By 1947, the dike was already very popular with fishermen. There was almost no time of day or night when someone was not out on the dike, crabbing or fishing. Although it is in Galveston Bay, the dike has even produced some trophy-sized deep-sea fish, including everything from large tiger sharks[1] to hammerhead sharks.

During the four years of World War II, the city grew in population from only 8,000 people to an estimated 18,000. Housing was scarce, wooden, and small. Some people described the town in that day as ramshackle houses surrounding giant refineries. Two-thirds of the housing was located within a mile of the refineries.

---

[1] The largest tiger shark caught off the dike was a 1004 lb. tiger shark in 2021.

Like most defense plant towns, the housing was small, but typical of the times. Post-depression housing was often planned in small subdivisions. The houses were usually owned by the employers and leased to their employees.

Most of the residential area was clustered immediately north of the industrial plants in a semi-circle. The city was bordered on the east and southeast by Galveston bay and on the southwest by tidal estuaries, shallow lagoons, and marshes. [2]

Texas City boasted thriving Catholic, Methodist, African Methodist Episcopal, and Southern Baptist churches. All of them had excellent clergy who would prove to be very valuable in the coming weeks and months. Most of the population were active Christian church members.

The west side of the city bordered on La Marque, an unincorporated town that had been around longer than Texas City, having been founded by survivors of the horrific 1900 Galveston Hurricane. La Marque appealed to those survivors as it boasted an average elevation of 13 feet above sea level. In comparison, Texas City's elevations ran from the water's edge to about 12 feet above sea level.

Texas City, including the plants, was less than 4 miles in diameter. After the war, Texas City continued to grow. By spring, 1947, there were about 25,000 people living in Texas City; and another 6,000 lived in adjacent La Marque. Unlike Texas City, La Marque had no industry and was seen as a 'bedroom community' for both Galveston and Texas City. Due to the housing shortage in Texas City in 1947, quite a few employees were forced to live in Galveston.

To travel from Galveston to Texas City required a drive of over 15 miles, even though the city was only about five miles directly north of Galveston, across a small neck of Galveston bay that included the Intracoastal Waterway. Most Texas City workers who lived in Galveston car-pooled. Some rode buses.

The lift bridge on U.S. Highway 75 over the Intracoastal Waterway had a two-lane roadway and dual railroad tracks. It frequently created traffic jams for Galveston residents if it was opened for ships during prime traffic times. To be at work on time, those who lived in Galveston had to allow at least an extra 30 minutes for the lift bridge, as it did not open or close on a regular schedule.

---

[2] See map before chapter 1.

It was no problem when the men arrived early for work. They simply waited in the various break areas, playing dominoes, until the morning whistle blew. That was what many of the men were doing at Republic Oil on the morning of April 16.

3

Republic Oil

ONE OF THE TYPICAL FAMILIES of Texas City in April of 1947 was a man named C.T. McCrocklin, his wife Marjorie and their three sons. C.T. and his family were some of those who lived through the disaster. It was much like living through a war of its own making, with no identifiable enemy.

Although C.T.'s family had ancestors in Texas from the time of Stephen F. Austin, he had been raised in Mansfield, Desoto Parish, Louisiana, about twenty miles from the Northeast Texas border. As a boy, C.T. lived through the great depression in Mansfield, with his mother and five siblings. Her only income was a Spanish American War widow's pension, so life had been sparse for the family of seven.

C.T. was 14 years old when the stock market crashed. He worked his way up in the refinery business. He began his career cleaning out old wooden crude oil tanks by hand in 1931, so that other petroleum products could be stored in them. It was a filthy job that he was glad to have at the time.

Because he held certifications as a bookkeeper, he was eventually transferred to jobs that required him to keep records of every ounce of product that flowed through the refineries where he worked. He was efficient and did a good job.

At the outset of World War II, C.T. and his family were living in Lawrenceville, Illinois, as he worked in the Texas Company[1] Refinery. While C.T. was working for the Texas Company in Lawrenceville, three sons were born to him and Marjorie. As the father of three sons and with a defense job, C.T. never had to serve in the military during the war. However, he did serve in the Illinois National Guard before the war and had honorably mustered out of the Guard only 2 months before the war began. Eventually, C.T. wound up in Texas due to the upheaval caused by the war. The Texas Company needed him in Port Arthur, Texas[2] more than it did in Illinois.

On January 2, 1943, with Marjorie and the boys, the youngest being six-weeks old, C.T. was transferred to Port Arthur by the Texas Company. The family traveled on a troop train with hundreds of soldiers who were on their way to Camp Polk in Louisiana.

C.T. worked in Port Arthur throughout the remainder of the war. He was a loyal American and was always proud of his efforts to support the soldiers. They joined the Baptist Church in Port Arthur and C.T. raised his family there, being faithful to worship each Sunday.

As soon as the war was over, C.T. received a promotion to a new job with Republic Oil Refinery in Texas City, Texas. In spite of the acute housing shortage in Texas City, the small family was glad to be there. They lived in a tiny and rather flimsy three-bedroom, one bath home, about 1½ miles from the refinery.

His new job was as the assistant plant manager of the Republic Oil Refining Company in Texas City. He was specifically in charge of union relations, employee benefits, and plant safety. He no longer counted barrels of petroleum. He reported directly to the plant manager, a man he truly liked, who had hired him away from The Texas Company.

The sole war-time product at Republic was aviation fuel for the government. Aviation grade fuel is a very special product that not all gasoline refineries can make. It requires high grade crude and special processing. All of Republic's wartime production was 110 octane aviation fuel. The refinery had been designed and built solely for that purpose.

---

[1] The Texas Company is known today as Texaco.
[2] Port Arthur is located thirty miles west of the Louisiana border.

The McCrocklin family home in La Marque.
Used by permission from Melissa Roberts.

After the war, however, some of that production was reduced to lower octane fuel by adding back specified amounts of kerosene in huge 300,000-gallon stirring tanks in Republic's #1 tank farm. That process had just begun in April of 1947.

The tank farms included two areas; Tank Farm #1 sat directly across the road from Republic to the west, and Tank Farm #2 was across the frontage road from Republic, to the southwest. Both tank farms were immediately adjacent to the refinery, across access roads.

Ten huge tanks, five in each farm, were each surrounded by earthen dikes, six feet tall. If the tanks burst, there was enough capacity in each of the ten diked areas to contain the stored liquids.

In 1947, Republic's primary customers shifted from the U.S. government to major and minor commercial distributors of gasoline. It sold products to the various Standard Oil companies, such as Humble Oil and Esso, as well as to Gulf Oil and Refining, The Texas Company, and the Sun Oil Company. Business was good. Republic and all the other refineries and chemical plants operated at full capacity.

There were only a few differences between what was pumped from a Texaco, Esso, or a Gulf filling station. In many places, the big-name labels were placed on Republic-produced products. C.T. and his brother George, who was an engineering and instruments man (E&I man) at Republic, were able to tell everyone they knew, "It's all gasoline; it doesn't matter where you buy it." The employees at Republic knew that all gasoline came from tanks like theirs and had the same amount of tetraethyl lead in them. C.T. had a full-page ad from Texaco about their gasoline framed in his office. He had placed a ribbon banner across it which read: "Proudly distilled by Republic Oil and Refining."

Like most refineries, Republic operated daily at full steam, except for one month each year when they went through 'turn-around.' Refineries are routinely shut down and refurbished as needed. Each year, many make a change over from gasoline to home heating fuels and back. Although there was no focus on home heating products at Republic, the general maintenance 'turn-around' usually occurred in July.

In 1947, Republic was one of the major employers in Texas City, along with Monsanto Chemical, Humble Pipeline, Atlantic Pipeline, Stone Oil Company, Sid Richardson Refining Company, Plancor Oil, and the Warren Petroleum Company.[3]

The plants were interspersed with hundreds of giant oil and chemical tanks, stills, connecting pipe lines and pumping stations, as well as pipe lines to the ship-loading stations at the port.

C.T. and George, like the other families in Texas City, loved their relatively high-paying jobs. Everyone who worked in Texas City was glad to have a job that paid well, since the returning were having trouble finding good jobs.

---

[3] See map, page 14.

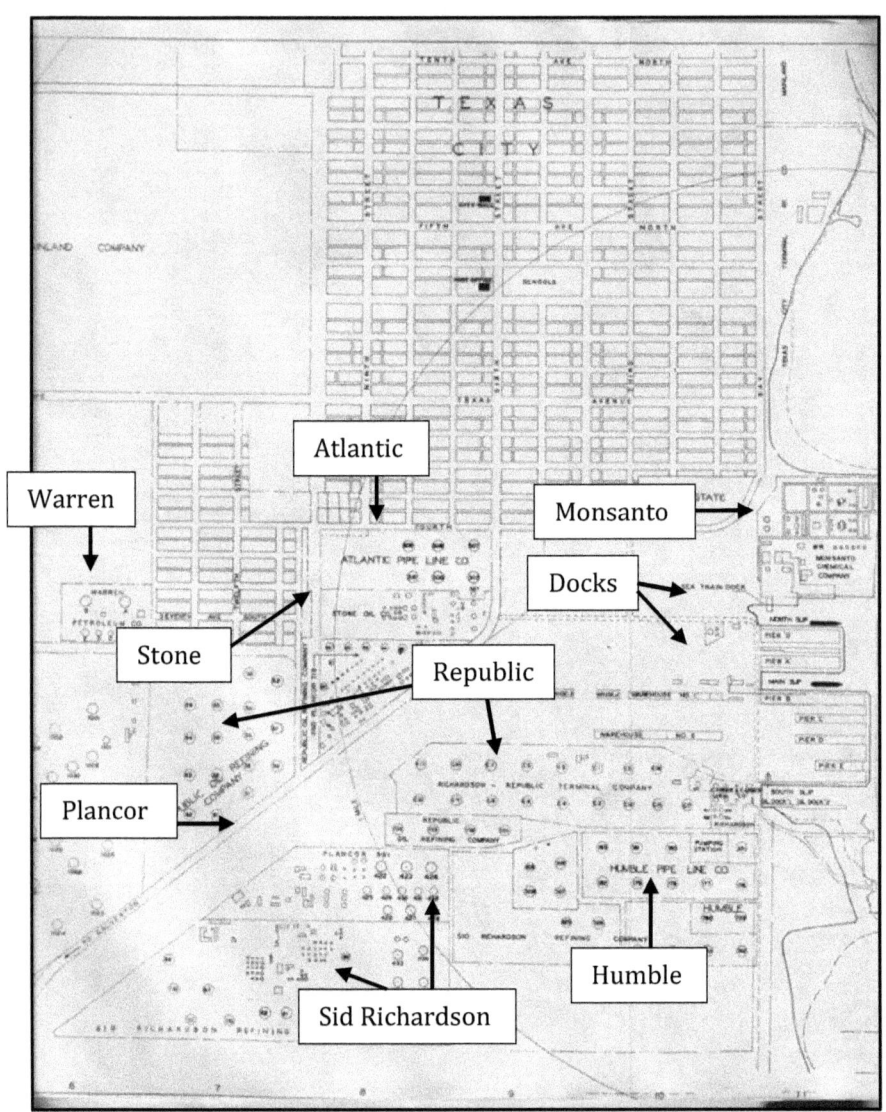

Texas City Refineries and Businesses, 1947. Used by permission from Fire Prevention and Engineering Bureau of Texas and the National Board of Fire Underwriters.

4

Prelude

Texas City, March 1947

THE TEXAS CITY TERMINAL RAILWAY Company owns and operates the port in Texas City to this day. They also owned the grain elevator at the port. The terminal railway supplied cargo to the ships in the port. Millions of tons of goods entered and exited through the port at Texas City. No one predicted how some of those goods would contribute to the horrific events of April 16, 1947.

The first of two ships, *SS Grandcamp*, was owned by the Republic of France and operated by *Compagnie Generale Transatlantique (CGT)*, commonly known as 'The French Line' and owner of the famous ocean liner, the *SS Normandie*. The second ship, the *SS High Flyer*, was owned by Lykes Lines of the USA. The *SS Grandcamp* was due to make port around April 6, 1947, but arrived at the dock on April 11.

The terminal president, Henry J. (Mike) Podesta, an experienced Texas A&M University Graduate Civil Engineer, saw nothing wrong with the planned shipment of fertilizer designated for the ships when it crossed his desk. The port had shipped other lesser amounts of fertilizer a few times before with no problem.

*The SS Grandcamp docked in Texas City circa 1940.
Used by permission from Houston Chronicle.*

He had no idea Houston had refused this shipment of fertilizer. As a civil engineer, he knew very little about chemicals, in spite of the fact that he routinely shipped vast quantities of petroleum products and the chemicals used to refine them.

Podesta did not question the shipping manifests. He reasoned that whoever had created them had done their job properly. He did not have time to question every manifest. He actually saw that as J.D. Lattimore's job.

J. D. Lattimore was the freight forwarder in charge at the time. He was known for his speed and what some people saw as unusual haste in forwarding shipments.

Podesta's main job was to keep the mechanical parts of the railway operating. He did not see it as his job to oversee the accuracy of shipment labeling. Although, he would have been hard pressed to say who should be checking each manifest, other than Lattimore.

Once the shipment was accepted and filed away in his office, Lattimore sat back and smoked a large Cuban cigar. He loved them very much and often had ship's captains bring him a box of duty-free '*Cubanos*' if they were in the Caribbean before coming to Texas City. Sometimes the captains did not charge him for the cigars, and he responded with an extra speedy turn-around for them. Perhaps his haste contributed to the impending disaster.

The fertilizer was shipped from three government-owned plants that had been temporarily converted from ammunition production to fertilizer after the war to aid Europe under the Marshall Plan. These ammunition factories, many of which returned to ammunition production for the Korean War and onward, were utilized due to the unpopularity of the Marshall Plan in the United States to avoid using U.S. fertilizer plants that were not controlled by the government. The fertilizer was packaged in the prescribed 100-pound, multi-ply, waterproof paper bags. 1947 shipping regulations allowed it to be packed in several types of shipping containers, all of them of cardboard or paper construction. It was supposed to be 32.5% ammonium nitrate, but it may have been shipped in concentrations as high as 38% ammonium nitrate. This occurred due to the higher concentrations of ammonium nitrate required for ammunition propellant and explosives. The extra 5.5% concentration, if it occurred, vastly increased its oxidizing properties.

The fertilizer being loaded on the ships was not properly labeled. It should have been labeled in bold letters as: "**OXIDIZER, FGAN, (Fertilizer Grade Ammonium Nitrate) 32.5%, in 100-pound paper bag.**" This would have told everyone handling it to know that it was very volatile and quite capable of burning without any air supply.

Oxidizers do not need air to burn. They supply oxygen for the other things being burned. In fact, it probably was thought to be inert by most of the men who transferred it. Since the word 'oxidizer' did not appear on any of the manifests and 'fertilizer grade ammonium nitrate' was only on one manifest, no one noticed or was aware that the entire shipment could burn violently. They certainly were unaware that the product could cause other flammable things to burn more viciously, even in an airless environment. They also were not aware of the product's low melting temperature of less than 300°F.

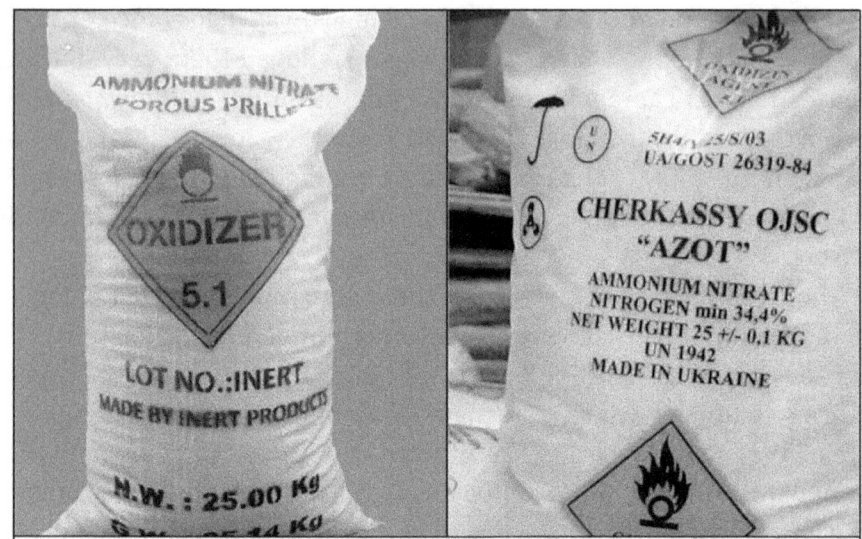

Correct labeling of Ammonium Nitrate Fertilizer. Used by permission from https://inertproducts.com and https://www.abc.net.

The three ordinance plants did not purposely mislabel the product, but they had been making military grade materials and not commercial grade fertilizer products, so the mistakes were reasonable, since they had no experience labeling and shipping FGAN. Their mistakes are not completely forgivable. They should have labeled the bags properly.

The fertilizer's intended purpose to revitalize the soil in Europe also necessitated a modicum of haste secondary to the upcoming planting season in France. None of the individual ordinance plants possessed the capability to fill such a large quantity on their own. All of this culminated in this shipment of fertilizer being manufactured/packaged in three separate locations, transported three separate routes, potentially labeled three separate ways and possibly in three separate concentrations.

The shipments were to be transferred from the rail cars to the warehouse at the dock, and then onto the ships by longshoremen. It was inevitable that some of the bags would tear and leak.

Shipping regulations required torn or leaking bags to be removed from any shipment before they could be loaded on ships. Those regulations, however, were universally ignored by the shippers and by the stevedores[1] that handled all cargo.

---

[1] A stevedore a person employed at a dock to load and unload cargo from ships.

Many regulations that had been adhered to very strictly during the war were quickly ignored afterward. Although illegal, shipping torn bags was commonplace. Mike Podesta made sure that plenty of cheap paper repair tape was always available to the stevedores he employed. He never knew if they used it or not. He should have noticed that his original supply never needed to be replaced.

Stevedores were paid by gross tonnage loaded, as well as by the hour. They saw no reason to waste time on closing leaking bags. As far as they were concerned, that was someone else's problem. Their goal was always to get the tonnage numbers up. If they had a lot of loose product, they simply shoveled it onto the pile of bags.

It did not bother Podesta because he saw it as a stupid regulation; one of those innumerable regulations imposed upon hard working men by bureaucrats. As far as Podesta was concerned, what mattered was that the product moved through the port quickly and efficiently. If some of it spilled, that was someone else's problem.

As a result, once loaded aboard the ships, all of the bags were coated with a layer of fertilizer, even when most bags remained sealed. If a tear in a bag could be folded over, as far as the stevedores were concerned, that was sealing it enough.

Some of the leaking bags were hastily taped closed with the cheap paper tape Podesta supplied and then stacked along with whole bags in the ships, filling the holds evenly from side-to-side and fore-to-aft. Most of the leaking bags were simply intermingled with the whole ones. The bags were stacked so that there was no more than 1" clearance between the stack and the curved hull of the ship.

The ship's crane would lower ten or more bags in cargo netting, into the hold; the longshoremen would manually stack them as tightly as possible to use up all available space in the hold. The job was to balance the load in every ship and to ensure it would not move around in rough seas. One cargo net of ten bags would be stacked on the port side and the next on the starboard. According to union rules stacking required two separate teams.

By April 15, the shipments had arrived in Texas City; they were initially stacked in the warehouse that ran down the middle of docks A-B and some was still being loaded on the two designated ships. In the process, many more bags were torn.

Loaded fertilizer in the hold of the SS Grandcamp. Used by permission from https://www.slideshare.net/slideshow/the-texas-city-disaster/238180602

The final 2,500-ton shipment of the fertilizer was still enroute to Texas City by rail from Iowa.

A combination of ignorance, haste in manufacturing and shipping, carelessness, mislabeling, mishandling, plus a lack of sufficient research testing by the chemical industry about the explosive properties of the product, was about to result in the worst industrial explosion in American history.

It is possible that some or all of the FGAN eventually shipped was around 38% in concentration. The entire production run was eventually destroyed, making any after-the-event testing impossible.

It should be noted that all ammonium nitrate (above 98.3% purity is virtually non-explosive, but it will melt and burn; lower concentrations than 98.3% purity when heated, pressurized, and in contact with petroleum products have been responsible for every FGAN explosion in history.

At 4:30 p.m. on April 15, the hatches were closed aboard both ships. No loading went on at night and both the *SS Grandcamp* and the *SS High Flyer* sat calmly at their moorings. The stevedores did not return until 8:00 a.m. on April 16.

On the morning of April 16, the *Grandcamp* was lying low in the water at the pier, indicating that she was almost fully loaded. Her name,

Grandcamp, was painted on her hull. The French Tri-color flag hung limply at her stern.

SS Grandcamp was a liberty ship built for World War II. She was 422 feet long, 57 feet abeam (width across the ship), 34 feet deep, and had five cargo holds. The five holds were separated by her midships house, the command center of the ship. Hold #4 was her mid-ships hold closest to the midships house.

She was built and commissioned in Los Angeles in 1942. She had a standard oil fired 2500-horsepower reciprocating steam engine. The fuel she normally burned in her engine was a heavy oil product called Bunker C. It was a viscous by-product of almost every refinery in the world; close to asphalt on the chemical tree, but still liquid at room temperatures. Her fuel tanks were full in preparation for the voyage to France. That fuel oil was to play a large role in the coming events.

Before she came to Texas City for her load of fertilizer, *SS Grandcamp* had loaded some cotton bales in Houston and sixteen crates of small arms ammunition. She also had 59,000 small, round, bales of pure sisal binder twine aboard. Those bales weighed about 25 pounds each.

She also had previously loaded 2,500 bales of tobacco as well as 2,500 bales of tobacco-in-leaf and 380 500-pound bales of compressed cotton. She carried drill stem and drill collars in some quantity. There also were 9,354 bags of shelled raw peanuts aboard that were loaded in Houston.

Her primary load was fertilizer. Texas City was to be her final stop before sailing for France. She would be fully loaded and was scheduled to sail on or before April 20.

Although not considered fast, as a liberty ship, she was known for her durability. Most sailors thought of liberty ships like work mules; that is, ugly, but strong and dependable. They were among the first completely welded steel ships in history, replacing costly and time-consuming riveting. In the beginning of World War II, German submarine warfare was devastating to allied Atlantic fleets, particularly toward supply and troop ships. In order to meet the supply demand, the United States industrial complex churned out 2710 Liberty ships between 1941 and 1945. Eighteen American shipyards produced these vessels at rate of nearly three ships completed every two days. The Liberty ships were crucial to the war effort.

Many people assume that all liberty ships were exactly alike. They were not. Various modifications of the basic design were allowed and produced. *SS Grandcamp* was known simply as a 'Liberty Model'.

Henry J. Kaiser envisioned, promoted, and was responsible for the Liberty ship. His genius in modular mass production put the USA ahead of every country in the world during the war years. The methods he developed of producing sections of a ship and then welding them to completed sections is still in use throughout the world.

The *SS Grandcamp* had served in the Atlantic Ocean from her commissioning. Her original name had been, *SS Benjamin R Curtis*. When she was sold to the French government for $1.00 after the war, she was then recommissioned as *SS Grandcamp*. (Some records show her name as *Grandecamp*.) Her stern and bow were painted with the name 'Grandcamp.'

After the war, she was mothballed for only a few months; and then after her purchase she was reflagged to the 'French Line' and was plying the Atlantic by late 1946, helping France to rebuild from the devastation of the war. This load of fertilizer would be used to revitalize the severely damaged farmlands of France. Her cargoes were usually mixed freight and she made several trips to and from Europe under the French flag.

SS Grandcamp had supplied the war and now was supplying reconstruction efforts in France. She boasted an adequate but not overly impressive engine. It could be said that her engines were simple standard steam engines of a type manufactured in the thousands before and after the day of turbines.

In the port of Texas City, there were two long piers that made up three docksides; docks O, and A/B. Sea Train owned some of the space at O dock. The A and B docks were about 700 feet long with corrugated steel warehouses placed continuously down the middle of the pier. *Grandcamp* was moored near the inland end of pier O, facing out, and east of the Sea Train crane.

Immediately behind and diagonally across the slip from *Grandcamp*, at piers A and B, *SS Wilson B Keene*, and *SS High Flyer*, American-flagged liberty ships, were also loading. Both of these ships were owned by Lykes Lines and managed out of New Orleans.

SS Wilson B Keene was a Liberty vessel with no particular type of designation. She was almost exactly the same size and power as

Grandcamp but had been built in Portland, Maine. The primary difference between the two ships was that the *Keene's* deck house was more forward than *Grandcamp's* midships deckhouse.

SS *High Flyer* had a very different design from the others. She boasted steam turbine propulsion, giving her much greater speed and overall performance. She was designated a 'Type C-2" vessel. She was 16 feet longer, 6 feet wider and considerably more powerful than the other two ships.

Manufactured in Los Angeles, she boasted a 6,000-horsepower steam turbine propulsion system. That made her twice as fast as *Grandcamp* and *Keene*. She could easily leave the port days after *Grandcamp* had embarked and beat *Grandcamp* to France. She burned fuel oil and not Bunker C.

She was scheduled to leave Texas City after the *Grandcamp* and to arrive before *Grandcamp* in France. *High Flyer* had previously loaded 2,000 tons of powdered Sulphur in Galveston. By the morning of April 16, 960 tons of FGAN had already been loaded. She was scheduled to load more dismantled wooden railroad cars for the needy French railways. Then, she would load additional FGAN. The reason for the staggered loading had to do with balancing the load. She was not loading fertilizer on the morning of April 16. As she had a later departure date, all the stevedores in port were concentrating on finishing *Grandcamp's* loading instead of continuing her loading.

The SS *High Flyer* was designed for high-speed travel across the vast Pacific. She had served well throughout the Pacific war. The three ships were sister ships only in that they were all Liberty ships. The moment she arrived in Texas City; *High Flyer's* turbine had its 25,000-pound cover removed for routine maintenance. As a result, she was a dead ship. However, that did not prevent her from being loaded, and she could sail as soon as the maintenance on her turbine was complete.

It was estimated that less than 25 more work hours would be needed on the morning of April 16 to have her turbine functional. The harbormaster was aware of her condition and had approved the maintenance to occur in Texas City. A fresh supply of high-quality Cuban cigars had accompanied the repair request. He had no way of knowing that *High Flyer's* lack of an operational engine would compound coming events. As a result of her maintenance, *High Flyer* was operating on shore power. *Grandcamp* and *Keene* kept their diesel generators running.

SS High Fligher (top), SS. Wilson B. Keene bottom. Used by permission from https://teshistory.unt.edu/ark:/67531/metapth11732/ and https://www.slideshare.net/slideshow/the-texas-city-disaster/238180602

The *Keene* was in port solely to load flour from the grain elevator. She would be a victim of the disaster, but she did not contribute to it. The loading of her cargo had only barely begun and most of her crew members were on brief shore leave.

She had loaded 40 tons of flour in cotton bags. Her loading was stopped due to the urgent need to load *Grandcamp* and *High Flyer*. There were not enough longshoremen available to load all three ships at once.

5

Orange Smoke

Texas City, Pier O

8:00 AM

SHIP REGULATIONS DID NOT PERMIT smoking in the hold, but throughout the ports of the world, smoking regulations were almost universally ignored. The *Grandcamp* had signs, written in French and posted throughout, ordering no smoking, but the crews ignored them.

Strict regulations imposed during WWII had become lax in virtually every port in the world. It seemed like the entire world was relaxing from wartime restrictions while trying to get on with reconstruction; additionally, the unions were flexing their muscles after they had been so restricted by wartime rules.

After the war, if men were ordered not to smoke, they simply walked off the job. Any delay was totally unacceptable for this shipment due to its urgent need in France.

The stevedores were smoking, mostly Camels or Lucky Strikes, ignoring the dull, painted French-language "No Smoking" signs. Somewhere during the loading process, one of the stevedores likely flipped a burning butt between the hull and the cargo.

At 8:02 am, smoke began rising from the ship's hull. A wisp of orange smoke rose between the hull and the cargo. The smoke quickly vented into the air above the open hold.

Due to the curve of the hull and the depth of the stacked bags, the bottom of the ship at that point was both invisible and unreachable. There was a 1-inch maximum clearance visible between the hull and the stacked cargo.

As C.T. and his brother George drove to work, they neared the front parking lot at Republic and noticed a very thin plume of brilliant orange smoke rising above the prominent, white-colored Sea Train facility gantry. The Sea Train gantry was immediately adjacent to the five-story synthetic-rubber-styrene factory at Monsanto Chemical Company.

Smoke began to rise above the ship. No one in Texas City had ever seen smoke of that color before. Most smoke from fires around chemical plants is very black due to the high amount of carbon in the flammables. This smoke was vibrant orange in color.

As C.T. and George drove the last few feet to work, the smoke rose higher and became a little more prominent in the azure sky. It was not much more than a wisp of smoke, but its color against the blue sky made it very striking. As the moments passed, the smoke increased in both size and volume. Somewhere, a fire was obviously getting a good start.

C.T. could not imagine what would burn with such brilliant orange smoke. The smoke was Halloween jack o' lantern orange. It was like the bright orange of a flame, but there were no flames visible. The column of smoke seemed to pulsate and glow from within as it began to swell in size.

As they reached Republic Oil in George's green, 1939 Desoto coupe, the thin column had risen to about 2,000 feet and began to flatten out into a mushroom shape. C.T. could not see the smoke's source. He wondered, "Is that fire burning at Monsanto's styrene factory, or at Sea Train?"

His concern only grew as the column slowly increased in size and intensity. It seemed strange to him that no flames were visible, only the bright, glowing and pulsating orange smoke.

C.T. asked George, "Have you ever seen smoke like that?" George was silent for a moment and replied, "I have never seen anything like that at all. I don't even know what is burning, but it sure is strange. In fact, it's a little ominous, don't you think, Tommy?"[1]

"I am totally bumfuzzled. It must not have any carbon in it to burn that color." said Tommy.

George replied, "My concern is how the smoke itself seems to be burning internally. Have you ever heard of smoke that burned?"

"No. I guess there must be particles in the smoke that have not yet burned when they rise above the source and are burning as we watch. I remember reading that a pyroclastic flow from a volcano is often red on the inside, but the outflow from those is always grey in daylight."

They pulled up to the refinery parking area and sat silently for about ten minutes, watching the column increase. George was finishing a Camel cigarette because there was no smoking allowed in most of the refinery. The pulsating orange smoke was gently wafting to the south across the A/B pier, but past that point it rose straight up in a pillar.

As they got out of the car, C.T. ended their conversation with, "Well George, as soon as I know what it is I will come down into the plant and let you know."

George stubbed out his Camel cigarette and headed to the time clock area to punch in for the day. C.T. did not smoke; he considered it an unnecessary waste of good money. Besides, he did not like the smell of cigarette smoke, although he always tolerated it from others, especially his brother.

C.T. stood in the parking lot for a few more minutes, looking at the smoke plume. He knew he needed to report in. Safety was one of his responsibilities. The single column of smoke did not seem to be spreading, only growing in intensity. Yet, the risk of fire in any chemical plant is always high. He did not want the fire causing this orange smoke to come across the narrow two-lane- road to Republic.

George went ahead and clocked in. It was 8:15 a.m. when C.T. entered the office building. He paused and looked at the view. The sky remained azure blue. The Sea Train gantry was pure white; and the nearby column of smoke was glowing orange. It was as beautiful as it was ominous.

---

[1] C.T.'s friends and family called him Tommy.

Sea Train was a company that facilitated the transfer of cargos of rail cars to ships and vice versa. It was easy to locate from a distance because it had the only large steel gantry on the dock. The 7-story gantry almost seemed to glow a brilliant white in the morning sun.

Entire railcars were loaded onto ships at Sea Train. It was the beginning days of the idea of containerized cargo. Sea Train was located at the terminus of the Texas City Terminal Railway Company, who owned the rest of the piers and docks.

C.T. grew more and more concerned about the close proximity of Monsanto Chemical Company's styrene facility. Humble Pipeline, Atlantic Pipeline, Stone Oil Company, Republic Oil Company, the Sid Richardson Refining Company, Plancor Oil, and the Warren Petroleum Company were exposed to the possibility of propagating fires. The potential was still remote, but the entire chemical complex in Texas City was threatened.

Arriving at his office, C.T. entered the ground floor of the office building immediately. That was not his normal entry, as his office was on the second floor and most easily reached from an outside steel staircase. He stopped at the receptionist and asked, "Jane, what is that column of orange smoke all about?"

She said, "I don't know. But it is a wild fire. That is for sure." Jane added, "The rest of the men from the office left on the company fire truck, about 5 minutes before you got here. They went to protect our av-fuel canning facility on the T-head on Pier A/B."

C.T. stood there for only a moment, thinking. He knew that his proper place was down at the T-head of pier A/B with the rest of the men from the office. At Republic, the men who were salaried office workers were trained in and assigned to fire duties and ran the company's fire truck. He was in charge of organizing the training which had been done by the Texas City Fire Department.

Republic owned one of only four fire trucks in the town, the other three belonging to the city. Blue-collar (union) refinery employees were expected to be needed to run the refinery, and shut it down, if necessary, in case of any fire. That meant that the six men from the Republic office were at the T-head.

Republic owned an oil-canning facility at the T-head. It had canned aviation gasoline during the war in 55-gallon drums. It was a valuable facility and C.T. knew that the men from the office had gone over to protect it from the threat of fire. That was all that the receptionist knew.

One of C.T.'s many duties was to be the safety representative for the refinery. That meant that he was in charge of all safety and fire suppression training. He was well-versed in the fire and explosion dangers the men faced at Republic and also was aware of the nearby chemical plants' large variety of products. He also saw to it that no one worked without a proper hard hat, gloves, and steel-toed shoes; and that eye protection was available everywhere in the plant.

He had studied many manuals and attended annual seminars about petroleum and chemical fires. C.T. had hosted safety and fire suppression training events for the other companies at Republic's cost.

He also knew that poisonous vapors might remain unburned in smoke and that they might linger long after a storage vessel or pressure vessel was evacuated. Even an empty pressure vessel, exposed to the open air for days, might still be explosive or poisonous, and was to be treated like a loaded gun.

He always inspected recently opened and ventilated storage tanks to see if they were safe to enter. Sometimes it took weeks of forced ventilation for a pressure vessel to become safe. During a fire, firefighters had to assume that not all vapors were being consumed.

C.T. wondered if the orange smoke was poisonous. He whispered a prayer that it was not. He asked God to protect the workers, his family, and himself. He did not know the appropriateness of that prayer.

Republic's fire truck had the ability to make and spray foam fire retardant, but only the newest fire truck in Texas City's fleet could also do that. It was not unusual in those days for only the Republic to have its own fire truck among the refineries and chemical companies.

The Texas City fire department owned three fire trucks, all pumpers, including a recently commissioned, brand new, $14,000 state-of-the-art pumper that had never seen service. It had been commissioned over the preceding weekend and had yet to go out on a call. For the duration of the war, the city and the plants had gotten by with two city trucks and Republic's lone pumper/foam truck.

If there were any liquid spills burning, the automatic plan was that both the city's trucks and Republic's truck would provide water and foam until they ran out of supplies. By then, it was hoped, help would be in place from Galveston, Houston, or both. C.T. was aware that the four fire trucks were all that existed in Texas City, in spite of the many chemical plants. The next nearest firefighting equipment was at least twenty miles away, in Galveston.

C.T. had a copy of the Galveston County disaster plan, which had been developed and maintained since the beginning of the war. It was a good plan based on possible espionage or naval attack.

The male Republic Oil office employees knew that they also could be called upon by any of the other chemical plants for assistance. They were prepared and trained to suppress any fire at any of the multiple Texas City plants. However, they were not trained to fight shipboard fires.

C.T. became well known for his strict adherence to no smoking rules at various places in the plant. C.T. did not smoke, and did not understand why the men were not satisfied with taking their regular smoking breaks in designated places, every two hours, as they worked. It seemed to him that 15 minutes to smoke every two hours, while being paid to work, was an ample benefit.

He was modestly proud of the plant's safety record, which was impeccable under his guidance. There had been no safety incidents at Republic since his arrival. The employees had reported only minor scrapes and bruises for over a year. C.T. personally managed the signs at the plant gates that read on April 16, "468 work days without serious accident." He changed the number each day. He was planning to put up '469' today.

After talking with the office receptionist, C.T. quickly jogged the half mile from his office to Pier A/B, heading to join his fellow office workers at the Pier A/B T-head canning plant. By the time he reached the parking lot for Monsanto, C.T. could see that it was a ship that was on fire. Her stern was facing him, and he saw the name *Grandcamp* and the French tricolor flag drooping from the staff at her stern.

Pier A/B was where the canning facility stood; and C.T. could see the company's fire truck at the end. Near the end of pier A/B, on the side labeled Pier A, the *SS High Flyer*, under American flag, was loading dismantled boxcars, directly across the slip from *SS Wilson B Keene*. *High Flyer* was floating higher in the water, so it did not appear to be nearly as fully loaded as *Grandcamp* and it was obvious that *Keene* was probably close to empty.

The fire did not appear to be spreading. By now, shimmering, orange-colored smoke was belching out of the forward midships hold of *Grandcamp*.

C.T. found his fellow office employees standing around watching the ship and the smoke, with their hoses charged and their pumper truck's engine running. The water was being sucked directly from the bay.

He greeted Texas City Fire Chief Henry Baumgartner by asking, "Are you going to put the new truck through its paces?"

Baumgartner replied, "Well, the Captain of the ship has not allowed us to put on any water or foam, so we are just here if it spreads or if he changes his stubborn French mind."

C.T. saw another friend, W. H. Sandberg, and greeted him. "Hi, Sandy. How are you?"

"Fine, Tommy. How are you?" Sandberg was the Safety Engineer for Monsanto and both he and C.T. had worked together at various safety seminars. They were not social friends but were close friends when it came to safety issues in Texas City.

"I am just fine; thanks, Sandy. How serious is this?"

"Well, Tommy, I just got here myself; from what I know, the product burning is fertilizer and cotton and sisal. The fire is contained to the ship, and we plan to keep it that way. I wouldn't normally be here today because I am supposed to be in North Texas. Some legal matters brought me home. However, I am glad that I am here so I can monitor this situation."

C.T. asked, "Sandy; I am on my way down to the canning plant and our fire truck. Do you need to send any messages that way?" "Yes. Tell your men that I hope they end up having nothing further to do; if the fire spreads tell them to jump on it and notify me only after they have already started to fight it." Sandberg added. "As for me, I am going back to my office unless this gets worse. Right now, it is up to the ship's captain,"

C.T. noticed that the only other fire trucks present were the Texas City Fire Department's three engines and what looked like their entire fire department of nearly 30 men. That meant that no help had been requested from Galveston or Houston. This was probably only a one-alarm fire.

The Texas City trucks were hooked up to the sole fresh water main on the pier; their hoses looked to be charged but were not pumping any water. They stood immediately next to *SS Grandcamp* with their charged hoses lying unused on the pier. Even if it had been a multiple alarm fire with the equipment, the professional and volunteer firemen from Galveston had been a mile away, they would not have been able to stop the coming events. The burning FGAN cargo did not need oxygen to melt and burn.

C.T. asked his boss, the plant manager, "What's burning in the ship? Sandy Sandberg wasn't completely sure."

His boss shrugged heavily and replied, "Fertilizer of some kind, Tommy."

C.T. knew from safety meetings with representatives of the other plants that no chemical fertilizer was made in Texas City. He correctly assumed that it had been transferred by stevedores to the warehouse from empty wooden MKT rail cars he saw sitting on the siding. When *Grandcamp* had arrived, loading had commenced from the warehouse. No freight was ever loaded directly from trains to ships. Sea Train was the only exception to that union rule.

C.T. knew nothing about this fertilizer, except that it obviously burned with a bright orange smoke. The lack of upper-level wind kept the smoke mostly in a column, with only a little wafting onto the piers. The smoke had a peculiar, almost sweet smell; but that was true of many chemical fires.

Republic's General Manager asked, "Tommy, do you think this is going to spread?"

C.T. searched his memory for the characteristics of chemical fertilizers and replied, "Probably not. All the fire is inside the ship. I don't see how it can spread through that steel ship onto this pier and then to our canning facility.

"I can see that they have unloaded some crates of ammunition. The crates of ammo are far enough away on the pier that they can be moved if the fire spreads beyond the dock. However, those balls of twine on the decks are something we should keep an eye on.

"If one or more of them is burning and falls onto this dock, we should not hesitate to extinguish it. Don't wait to ask for permission. This wooden dock is soaked with old spills. "You might want to make some foam, just as a preliminary precaution.

"What bothers me is that this is a very hot fire, and I have never seen any smoke like this. It looks downright evil to me. But it looks like we may just have to stand-by until the cargo all burns out." After a pause he added, "Fertilizer is often flammable and some of it will burn viciously, but it will not explode; so there probably is not much danger of the fire spreading. This all might be over in an hour or two."

C.T. paused and added, muttering, "We must keep the fire from spreading at all costs. May God help us if it spreads." There was another pause before he asked, "Has any water been put on it?"

The GM replied, "Not that I know of; we certainly haven't used our hoses. The captain would have to give us permission to put water on his ship.

6

Fire

Texas City, Dock A/B

8:50 AM

C.T. SAID, "I AM GOING to see if I can go onboard and look at it from above. After that, I really ought to go back to my office. I have an appointment with an insurance representative about increasing the coverage on our tank farms. I don't think it would be wise to cancel that appointment because of a fire down here."

C.T.'s manager gave permission as he replied, "OK, Tommy. There doesn't appear to be much to do here; but you stand by. We will watch for any spread of the fire. I will send for you if we find that we need you."

C.T. turned, went to the gang plank, and climbed unchallenged up to the midhouse above the main loading deck for a better view. The ship was surprisingly devoid of men. C.T. could see the captain and another officer watching from the command deck above him in the midhouse.

No water was being poured into the hold by anyone; including the Texas City firemen, but C.T. assumed that they knew best; and he assumed that they did not expect water to have much potential for a good effect. The ship was sitting absolutely still, as it belched ever growing quantities of orange smoke.

As the brilliant orange smoke increased in volume, the wooden hatch covers lay next to the open holds. No men got near the smoke plume. C.T. felt the fierce heat through his clothes and even his shoes. He wondered how long it would be that he could continue to stand here. He lifted each foot and examined the soles of his shoes.

They were leather, so the soles did not melt; but his right shoe sole was smoking a little. He began to alternately stand on one foot at a time. He mused, "This is a new dance called 'The *Grandcamp* shuffle.'"

By 8:58 a.m. the water in the slip around the hull had begun to boil. When it was shouted that the water was boiling, C.T. looked over the side of the ship. What he saw was like a reverse iron kettle, with the fire on the inside and the boiling water on the outside.

C.T. knew that the boiling water would probably keep the steel exterior of the ship from melting, but he wondered just how hot the fertilizer inside was getting to be. The steel hull had to be at least 300° for the seawater touching it to boil. In fact, the hull was probably closer to 700°.

He did not know that the fertilizer melted at only 265°. He also did not know that if even a small amount of petroleum product touched the molten fertilizer the result would be an instantaneous major explosion.

The situation was obviously becoming desperate. C.T. did not realize how desperate everything already was. The choking smoke had quickly made it impossible to work in the hold. The First Officer, acting as the officer in charge, had previously ordered a ship's fire hose to be unrolled and lowered partially into the hold. He intended to flood the hold and thereby extinguish all the fire. Before he could order the hose to be charged and turned on, the ship's captain, Captain Charles de Guillebon, countermanded his order. The brief argument was in French, but C.T. assumed that de Guillebon was concerned with damaging the unburned cargo.

C.T. was right in his assumption. However, only completely covering the burning fertilizer with water would have extinguished it. It needed to be cooled closer to room temperature to become stable.

The hose was left dangling in place, but no water was allowed to flow. No water was put on the fire in its initial stages and no water was used now that the fire was obviously getting vicious.

That was the last missed chance to put out the fire. Flooding the hold would have cooled and smothered it enough to put out the fire. No one onsite had any idea that only complete immersion would extinguish the molten FGAN.

As C.T. watched, he realized that there was a complete lack of communication between the ship and the shore. He was fascinated by the scene and the scarce attempts to extinguish the fire.

Captain de Guillebon ordered a last-ditch effort to put out the fire. He ordered the hatches to be sealed, (once closed, the hatches were covered with tarps, and wet down to prevent most of the smoke and any flames from exiting.) Captain de Guillebon hoped to smother the fire.

He also ordered live steam to be pumped through the hold's fire suppression system to help smother the fire. That was a standard practice for smothering marine fires that could not be extinguished in any other way onboard merchant ships.

De Guillebon hoped that the steam would not destroy any of the remaining cargo; but he saw no other option. It was a firefighting technique that was only used when merchant captains no longer felt that any of their cargo could be saved by any other method. As a result, however, things only got worse, although they briefly appeared to be better. The live steam melted even more of the FGAN.

The pressure in the ship's hold increased dramatically and the smoke column abated almost entirely. Was the fire possibly being smothered? There was minor cheering from both the ship and the crowd onshore.

The other holds on *Grandcamp* had several vents that began leaking smoke, and curiously that smoke was now very black. Captain de Guillebon ordered those vents to be sealed with wet tarpaulins, too.

C.T. wondered what had caused the change in color. "Maybe the steam was smothering the fire and the resulting smoke was black?" He did not realize that the black smoke may have indicated a rupture in a Bunker C fuel-oil tank or supply line. When the burning fuel oil reached the molten FGAN, the chain reaction would inevitably begin.

C.T. noticed a large crowd of people watching the fire from the area along Monsanto's northern security fence and others that he personally knew were parked or standing nearby, attracted to the peculiar orange smoke like moths chasing a candle flame. The crowd of curious people was growing, and that also concerned him.

An onshore breeze had sprung up and was now moving the black smoke to the north. The original orange smoke was now a truncated column in the stiller air above the onshore breeze.

C.T. saw two airplanes circling the truncated orange pillar, quite lazily, and they also drew his attention. With the absolutely clear conditions, and the brilliant orange smoke still hanging in a column in the air, it was in every sense a menacingly beautiful sight. The orange against the azure sky looked as if it had been painted on by the Master's hand.

One of the planes was painted a bright yellow color, making it even more visible. C.T. assumed that the airplanes were probably photographing the event and he assumed so correctly.

He also heard the order to close hatches and add smothering steam given by the Captain. The order was given in broken English and French, but C.T. understood it clearly. He saw about eight crewmen come out of the forecastle and begin moving the hatch cover materials.

C.T. trotted down the gangplank and walked around the scene before heading back to his office, which was less than half a mile away. As C.T. walked, he was not afraid; everything seemed to be well in hand. He whistled absent mindedly, indicating some inner nervousness, as he rarely ever whistled when he was not nervous. He even stopped and greeted a few of the people he knew.

He saw Sandberg again and said, "Sandy, this is looking serious." Sandberg replied, "Yes, it is, I may evacuate Monsanto."

He saw Jim, his across-the-street neighbor, who worked at Monsanto. "Hi, Jim." "Hi, Tommy." Jim was sitting in his 1938 Chevrolet Coupe in the first row of the parking lot. C.T. leaned on his open car door and asked, "You waiting to go in to work?" Jim replied, "Yeah. Watching this burn is more fun than reading gauges. Besides, I may see something that everyone else wants to talk about later." "See you later Jim." "Yeah; Bye Tommy."

SS Grandcamp and *SS High Flyer* both already held very large amounts of ammonium nitrate fertilizer. 2/3 of the total shipment was in Texas City. The rest was still in route, consigned to the *High Flyer*.

Since she was only loading box cars, the 25 hours of work still needed to make *High Flyer*'s turbine operational was not considered important. It left her a sitting duck for further disaster.

C.T. also knew nothing of the history of ammonium nitrate fertilizer or how dangerous the FGAN was about to be proven to be. It was known to burn, furiously at that, but its explosive properties had been overlooked by authorities.

He also did not know that two of the bills of lading under which it was shipped were incorrectly labeled as to its oxidizing properties. No one at the site knew that it would burn readily without any oxygen.

(After the events of April 16 and 17, FGAN was immediately reclassified as a potent explosive. Testing established that if you heated it to melting point and added only a small amount of petroleum product to it, it became similar in power to TNT.)

It was later assumed that Bunker C fuel oil from the *SS Grandcamp* had somehow mingled with the burning and molten fertilizer under steam pressure, and the entire load was certain to detonate. There is no record that any FGAN has ever been shipped through Texas City again.

SS Grandcamp also had the sisal twine and other things on her decks and in her holds, including bales of cotton. *SS High Flyer* had 700 tons of powdered sulfur in her holds, and the 900 tons of ammonium nitrate was stacked in bags on top of the sulfur.

No one knows to this day how the fire began. It has been assumed by authorities that a stevedore or a crew member dropped a burning cigarette among the paper bags of fertilizer.

As the fire grew in intensity, more people, both the curious and the ones who came to help fight the fire gathered. Many stood less than one quarter mile away, with nothing but a chain link fence between them and the ship. It is estimated that more than fifty men, women, and children were watching through the chain link fence.

Their discussion ranged from, "What is burning?" to "Is Monsanto on fire? My husband works over there." The crowd mostly just stared in rapt attention, conversing in low tones among themselves.

The city's residential area started immediately behind their backs, across the two-lane perimeter street that separated Monsanto's property from private properties. None of them could have known that over two blocks of houses to the north of them would be completely demolished in a few minutes.

C.T. returned to his office. He wanted to be on time to his meeting with the insurance agent. C.T. was the last known person to leave the immediate scene alive. Death was about to close its merciless hands on hundreds of people; but C.T. would be spared because of an appointment that soon proved useless.

C.T. later said, "I think I know exactly how the people of Israel in Egyptian exile must have felt when the Angel of Death flew over their blood-marked houses. He certainly flew right over me several times during the disaster. "

C.T. waved or nodded at over 30 people in the parking lot as he made his way west through the lot. They were all acquaintances, and their faces would be burned into his memory by coming events.

7

The Gates of Hell

AT 9:12 AM, C.T. TOOK one last look at the fire scene and entered his two-story office building from an outside staircase and closed the steel outer door. He did not quite have the door closed when the ship disintegrated into millions of pieces. The door was wrenched from his grip and flew open.

C.T. was knocked to the floor and later discovered that his hearing was seriously and permanently damaged in his right ear, because it faced the blast. He never did meet with the insurance representative. The man is assumed to have left the scene immediately.

The explosion occurred sometime between 9:12 and 9:17 am. Most local clocks were stopped by the explosion, indicating 9:12. The April 24 official report of the U.S. Coast Guard's Board of Investigation recorded the explosion occurred at 9:15 a.m.

Regardless of the exact time, in less than one second, more than 550 people were alive, and a millisecond later they were hurled into eternity. Many were simply vaporized, and nothing was ever found of them. Before all the events were over, up to 20,000 people would be injured.

The explosion was filmed by a woman standing on the Texas City dike, about a mile or two away. The orange smoke had drawn her attention. She was using 8mm color film, and the explosion was so bright that it whited-out the entire film stock. She was knocked down by the concussion and her filming ended. She survived with minor cuts and bruises.

*The Texas City Port before the explosion.
Used by permission from the Houston Chronicle.*

The post-explosion smoke was now boiling black, with no sign of the orange smoke remaining in the sky. The resultant fires produced roiling black clouds that spread out over Texas City and over Galveston Bay. The smoke column was seen from downtown Galveston.

The initial concussion was felt and heard in Houston, forty miles away, and was felt through the ground as far away as Gueydan, Louisiana, an oil town on the Intracoastal Waterway. Gueydan is a straight-line distance of over 130 miles east of Texas City. A local Gueydan barber felt the concussion under his feet and heard the ten-foot-long mirror behind him crack. He left that cracked mirror in place for at least ten years as a testimony to the force of what happened in Texas City. The blast was so powerful, it registered on a seismograph in Denver, Colorado as an earthquake, over 900 miles away.

The Monsanto Plant on fire. Used by permission from the Houston Chronicle.

Only those watching before the explosion remember the orange smoke. For most people, the Texas City Disaster is remembered as a huge series of explosions and boiling cauldrons of black smoke that rose from hundreds of sources all through the chemical plant district.

In just a split second, the fertilizer exploded. The force was initially contained by the steel hull of the Grandcamp and was directed outward and upward by the water of the boat slip. However, no steel ship's hull could hold this force, and within milliseconds it burst out in a great gush of heat and concussive force.

The white-hot expanding gasses completely consumed the FGAN in less than two thousandths of a second. Most of *Grandcamp* above the water line was obliterated. Her stern flew into the air and was deposited between the dock and the Monsanto building. Her anchor was blown nearly one-half mile away. Most of her hull and superstructure now existed only as white-hot shrapnel. Except for part of her stern, most of the remains of the SS Grandcamp were never identified, although hot chunks of steel were scattered in a five-mile radius. At least half of the steel remains of the ship are thought to have fallen into Galveston Bay, although some chunks of steel may have flown completely over the southern end of Galveston Island.

The men from Republic at the fire truck did not have time to react. One minute they were watching the ship and the next second, they were vaporized. Captain de Guillebon never knew that his decision to not flood the hold had signed his own death warrant.

Within three seconds, fully 1/3 of the residential housing in Texas City was either destroyed or damaged. The six block-square of housing immediately north of the Monsanto property was completely demolished. Three-to-four entire city blocks of wood frame houses behind them were also either totally destroyed or made uninhabitable. The streets remain uninhabited to this day.

In La Marque, a small lad was playing in his back yard. He felt the concussion come through the ground and stood still. Then, the boy heard a whistling noise and three pieces of drilling stem, each twenty feet long, stuck into the yard at a 30-degree angle, burying themselves six feet into the ground. He looked at them and yelled for his mother at the top of his voice. He screamed, "Help! Help! Help!"

The *SS High Flyer* was not burning, but she was severely damaged. The superstructure, crew quarters, and command decks were wrenched and broken. Her hatches had been battened, covered with tarps and wet down. They were still closed. Fire was not noticed onboard the *High Flyer* until around 6:30 that evening.

SS Wilson B Keene was also severely damaged above the water line. She was on fire, but not badly. She had been loading broken-down rail cars and was not loading FGAN. The floor in her hold was not afire.

Both remaining ships were torn from their moorings and ended up resting alongside each other, bows to sterns. No one that had been exposed on either ship was visible.

C.T. did not know what had happened. He may have been knocked out for a few seconds. Since the outside door was blown open, as he staggered to his feet, he was able to see the raging fires at Monsanto. With total shock and awe, he watched as multiple burning bales of sisal twine and white-hot pieces of steel fell in a wide arc all around him. It was raining fireballs like a scene one might expect from Dante's *Inferno*.

Monsanto on fire (right) along with the oil refineries. Note the proximity of the neighborhoods to the fire. Used by permission from the Houston Chronicle.

Storage tanks full of gasoline and other petroleum products were beginning to explode and burn in a two-mile-wide semi-circle. As C.T. looked around, he could see secondary fires at every chemical company in the area. Most important was the absolute inferno where the piers and Monsanto had been. Amazingly to C.T., the Sea Train gantry stood in stark white contrast to the red flames and black smoke boiling all around it.

Monsanto's synthetic rubber plant had been a concrete structure with five stories of multi-paned glass windows. It had become a burning concrete shell.

It was hard to believe, but C.T. was certain that everyone at the site and most in the burning styrene plant and for quite a distance around the site had been killed. He could not know, but eventually, sixty-three unidentified bodies and parts of bodies would be buried in a common grave, and that a total of over 180 people would never be found at all.

The remains of a fire truck, which had been blown across the docks and partially landed on a barge. Used by permission from the Houston Chronicle.

W. H. Sandberg was far enough away to survive. He had been hit in the head with some small shrapnel. He became famous for his efforts of directing the recovery and for his unsmoked Cuban cigar stub clamped in his mouth under his bandage-covered head.

No one from C.T.'s office that was on the T-head of the pier survived the initial explosion. It is to be assumed that all were vaporized, along with the ship, the crew, the stevedores, and all but one of the entire Texas City fire fighting force.

The only reason that a lone Texas City fireman was not on scene was because Fire Chief Henry Baumgartner had told him to go home because he had already stood duty all night. All firefighting equipment available within 20 miles was obliterated. Three of the four trucks at the scene were not visible, or else their wreckage was unrecognizable.

Many individual ruptures, fires and explosions followed the initial blast, some only by milliseconds. Both the size and the numbers of fires were growing exponentially.

White hot steel was flung in a large radius estimated to be from three- to-five miles. A huge empty liquid sulfuric acid barge, *Longhorn II*, was lifted by the accompanying tidal wave and deposited 100 yards inland. It was thought that the concussion drove her down in the water and the resulting 15-foot tidal wave then lifted her ashore.

*Downtown Texas City on the afternoon of the explosion.
Used by permission from the Houton Chronicle.*

The *Wilson B Keene* was listing. The *SS High Flyer* was not on fire, and the pier and warehouse next to the SS *Keene* and the *SS High Flyer* were mostly either destroyed or burning. Unloaded FGAN in the warehouse burned furiously but did not explode.

The people watching from behind the chain-link fence bore the full concussive force of the explosion. They were all killed instantly. The concussion alone collapsed their internal organs.

Before noticing anything else as the explosion occurred, eyewitnesses saw both circling airplanes as they were crushed; killing their pilots and passengers, and the remains fell straight to the earth from an estimated 1,000 feet in the air. It was if a big fist had risen up to them and wrung them into the wreckage.

The planes' destruction was the first sign of the explosion as the shock wave reached them first. Observers saw them fall straight down as tattered wreckage, not able to discern any bodies as they fell. A total of 4 men were later found to have died in the planes.

As dazed people made their way out of damaged and destroyed downtown businesses, one of the men on the street saw a young child, a preschooler of about four years old, making his way slowly out of the remains of the collapsed houses. The child was holding his entrails that were exposed on his abdomen as he picked his way through the wreckage.

The man began to run toward the child, but the boy saw him, got a startled look on his face, and turned back into the wreckage. Try as he might, even though he made a frantic search, the would-be rescuer never found the child. The young boy was just one of over 550 people who died that day. His identifiable remains were not found for days.

The grain elevator, holding the flour expected to be loaded on the SS *Keene*, was a solid reinforced concrete structure of about five stories in height. It stood about one-half mile from the boat slip. It did not burn; but it was so badly damaged internally that it became useless.

All the grain elevator employees were killed, including one man who was outside. He had been leaning against the concrete outside wall of the grain elevator, probably watching the fire when *Grandcamp* exploded.

He was crushed when a steel exterior door slammed him against the side of the elevator. Decades later, the grain elevator was eventually demolished.

Around 9:16 a.m. by his watch, C.T. was standing on the outside steel stairway to his office that he had just used to enter the office. He clung tightly to the railing and watched in shock as the destruction continued.

All around him he could see the black smoke of burning structures. White hot steel fragments and burning sisal bales and even some burning cotton bales were still falling like diffused rain.

Then C.T. saw a lone man running, toward him, and away from the inferno at Monsanto. The man was covered with black soot, oil, or both, but he did not look burned. His clothes had been completely blown off by the explosion. He didn't even have on shoes or socks. C.T. was amazed as he watched the man come toward him. He had never seen anyone run faster.

Then he realized that the naked man was running straight at a chain link security fence that was on the west side of Republic's property. It was a six-foot tall fence, with a triangle of barbed wire topping it. The man's trajectory would take him in front of the office building where C.T. stood, and from there, straight into the fence. As the man approached the fence, C.T. came out of his benumbed stupor. He held up his arms and yelled at the top of his voice, "Look Out!"

The grain elevator. Used by permission from the Houston Chronicle.

The naked man either did not hear him over the sounds of explosions and fires, or else he was so shocked himself that he did not care; he hurdled the almost seven-foot-tall structure like it was a low railing. He ran off to the northwest, away from the carnage. C.T. never saw the man again. It would have been amusing, if it had not been so pathetic.

C.T. vomited convulsively. He vomited several times more until he thought his stomach would turn inside-out. It was not to be the last time he would vomit over the coming days and weeks. He was very sensitive to motions and to odors, all his life. After he was through vomiting, C.T. turned and ran inside the building. He found all the secretarial staff to be alive. He told them to stay inside until he got back to them. Most ignored him and ran out the front door to see what was going on. Some of them immediately returned indoors. That allowed C.T. to turn his attention to the rest of the Republic facility.

He could see three huge tanks in the tank farm burning furiously and he dismissed them from his mind. He hoped the earthen dikes around each of them would function as designed and contain the burning aviation fuel.

*Further damage from the SS Grandcamp explosion.
Used by permission from the Houston Chronicle.*

He thought how ironic it was that they were burning at the very moment he was supposed to be arranging for increased insurance coverage for them. He also knew that there was no way the fires would be extinguished under the circumstances. Some of the fires in Texas City were to burn for weeks.

C.T. ran upstairs to his office and looked for his hard hat. When he could not find it, he hurried down the intact exterior staircase and within twenty yards met his brother, George, who was day foreman of the refinery's E & I men (Engineering and Instrument). The E&I were the men who turned every valve in the plant.

C.T. yelled to him, "Shut the plant down." He knew that it was a process of several days' duration to stop all the flow through a large gasoline refinery. The sooner shutdown was begun, the sooner it would be finished. He wanted the first valve to be turned off and was sure that his brother

George knew exactly which valves to turn off, and in what order, to completely shut down the refinery processes. He did not know of anyone else on scene that would have the slightest idea how to shut down the production stream of volatile and even poisonous gasses and fluids, including himself.

George asked, "What happened? What caused this?" C.T. replied, "Fire, in a French ship called *Grandcamp*! She must have blown up! Get us shutdown!"

They had to yell over the sounds of concussions and screaming flames coming out of severed pipelines. George turned away and began looking for any other E & I men to give them orders.

George's next few weeks would be consumed with closing and then eventually restarting the refinery processes. He went about his dangerous tasks with great courage.

C.T. quickly toured the entire refinery property and saw that the union men were putting out small fires and stopping leaks quite well.

Except for the tank farm, Republic Refinery was in fairly good condition, all other things considered. It was very important that the refinery's huge tank of hydrofluoric acid was not breached. That acid, if it had become an aerosol, could have killed thousands. It appeared that most of the molten chunks of steel had flown over the plant, first falling in the tank farms beyond the facility. Unless the fires spread into the main plant, C.T. was confident that it would be operable again in a week or two. The question would remain as to where to store crude oil and gasoline, since the tanks farms were burning.

C.T. did not know what would happen next; but for the moment the disaster at Republic Oil was contained. All around him outside his plant there was nothing but total chaos.

Many of the newer employees of the plants were military veterans; and they were the kind of men who took necessary actions and then asked for permission. They proved to be of tremendous help.

The survivors were now organizing themselves into small work parties and handling the crisis as best they could, with whatever equipment was at hand. All union rules about the duties of pipefitters versus carpenters, etc., were overlooked in the coming days.

Everyone who worked in the plants in Texas City knew the hazards and dangers of working with petroleum and other chemicals. Not one of them could have imagined a disaster of this scale. While it was assumed that fires *could* spread from plant-to-plant, no one had envisioned all of the plants with fires within 20 seconds. In every chemical plant, there were heroic acts by equally committed men. C.T. did not see his brother George again for several days. Both were very busy.

He stood very still for a minute or two, thinking out loud to no one in particular, "What do I do next?" Then he remembered to pray. "Father, your Word says, 'even though I walk through the valley of death, I will fear no evil.' Help me to be brave and to rescue people, if possible. Look after my family until and after I get to them. In Jesus' Name, I pray, Amen."

The realization that he was now the company's senior employee on site was sobering. He was certain that everyone on the ship, the pier, the T-head, and nearby, was dead. He was conflicted with whether he should stay on site at Republic or if he should try to help more closely to the original explosion.

It was around 9:20 am, only five-to-eight minutes after the initial explosion, that C.T. made up his mind and grabbed a stretcher and a very few first aid supplies from the plant's emergency supplies room and headed toward Monsanto and the very center of the inferno.

He was dressed in his normal gabardine work slacks, a white shirt complete with a maroon and grey tie, black dress wing-tip shoes, and a grey fedora hat. It would not be long before he would shed the shirt and tie as they became coated with blood, oil, human remains, and soot. He spent most of the coming day and evening in his slacks and his originally white, sleeveless, top under shirt.

At first, no one was in charge. Individuals became groups of two, three, and eventually four men. Then Sandberg took charge. He set up a control area just west of the Monsanto property on Terminal Railway land, in the middle of a road. It would later be the location of one of the memorials to the disaster.

C.T. ran up to him, noticed his bleeding head, and yelled at the top of his voice over the screams and explosions, "Stand still; I can clean-up your head!" Sandberg looked shocked, felt his forehead and saw that his hand came away bloody. He sagged a little and allowed C.T. to clean his head with tincture of iodine and to wrap it in a clean bandage. Sandberg did not even wince as the iodine was applied.

He then asked C.T., "Tommy? Are you okay? I thought you were probably killed."

"No, I'm not hurt; what do you want me to do?"

Sandberg looked around and said, "I guess someone has to go into that hellfire and look for people. Can you do that?" C.T. replied, "I will try." Sandberg asked, "How are things at Republic?"

"The refinery is going to be okay. I cannot say anything good about our tank farms. Some of the tanks are still okay. Half of them are burning."

Since he had a folding stretcher, C.T. found three other men whom he did not know and asked them to help look for survivors. They agreed, and the foursome plunged into the still-exploding inferno, with C.T. carrying the lone folded litter.[1]

Before they plunged into the inferno, C.T. led them in a prayer that was simple and short, "God help us!" There was one emergency team, with one litter, that was the first into the inferno. C.T. headed it up, constantly repeating, "God help us. God help us."

Sandberg looked at his broken off cigar stub and clamped it in a vise-like mouth. That Cuban cigar did not leave his mouth, except for when he drank water, for the rest of the day.

Fires were burning everywhere, with that peculiar extreme screaming hiss that only escaping and vaporizing high pressure liquid petroleum products can make.

Every car in the Monsanto parking lot was destroyed and many were on fire. C.T. planned to lead his crew through wreckage and flames until they found someone alive. They hoped to find injured people so that they could rescue them. Few people were found alive. The few still living were the first people they removed.

More often than not, C.T. and three other volunteers would eventually load a dead body on their stretcher, find something to cover it, if they could, and work their way back out through the fires and wreckage. One of the problems C.T.'s team faced was the way flames would flare out from a source, recede, and then suddenly flare again.

---

[1] A litter is is a lightweight stretcher with sides and a removable head covering. It is used to transport injured people in situations where movement is limited, such as in confined spaces, on slopes, or in dense forests.

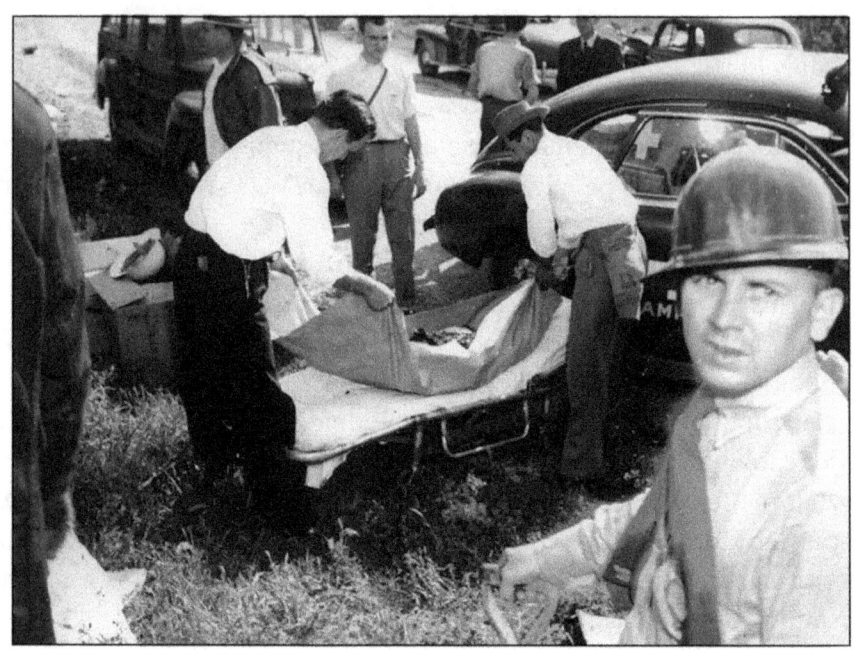

Recovering bodies. It is believed that C.T. is center left, wearing a white long-sleeve shirt without a hat. Used by permission from the Houston Chronicle.

If an above ground pipeline was completely severed, the flames often made 30-foot-long jets, ten feet in diameter. Below-ground-pipelines shot flames up through the earth in wider jets of fire, making the soil itself boil.

Occasionally the team brought out a living victim; but only occasionally. Some of the dead were women who had worked in the offices at Monsanto. Many had their clothes completely blown away. They had a hard time finding tarps sufficient to cover their bodies to give them some dignity in death. C.T gave up his previously white shirt to cover one woman.

Soon they became an efficient team. They thought of their work as 'rescue' work, but in truth it was almost entirely 'recovery' work from the beginning. They had no work gloves, protective helmets or other protective gear. C.T. initially wore his fedora, until he lost it somehow avoiding some explosive flames. He watched it fly into a burning jet of flames. It just flared briefly and disappeared.

*Damaged cars in the parking lot.
Used by permission from Houston Library System.*

Sandberg found C.T. a hard hat on his return to the crisis control area, saying, "Tommy, we need your brain and your knowledge. Keep your head protected."

Access paths through the flames and wreckage that were available at any given time were closed by fire only a few moments later. That meant that every trip into the area was a frustrating action of going one way, falling back, and trying for another. Explosions were continuing all around the rescuers.

In a short amount of time there were multiple teams of volunteers who joined in the rescue efforts. It was to be nearly 45 minutes before the Coast Guard and a group of volunteers arrived from Galveston.

That was a quick and efficient response for Galveston County authorities and the Coast Guard. The first Galveston contingent brought four city buses with them. They were intended for use as ambulances, but as it was to turn out, three of the busses immediately became hearses for the coroners at John Sealy Hospital. The fourth remained in Texas City as an ambulance.

Someone found some potable water and there was a little to drink every time they returned with a filled stretcher. At this point they were limited to recovering only wounded people or whole bodies. There were many body parts lying around that they simply passed by.

C.T. reasoned that they could not waste their efforts on a leg, an arm, a torso, or even a head. Those parts could be recovered later.

It was nearly 10:00 a.m. when they first reached the Monsanto parking lot. It was a crushed and burned-out junk yard. C.T. told his men, "Let's check four cars at a time. Each of us will be responsible for one car. If the car still has a door, leave it standing open as a sign the car has been checked." In order to be heard over the screaming escaping gasses, they got into what looked like a football huddle before each search of four cars. C.T. took the role of quarterback. At each huddle, he took time for prayers of thanksgiving and for God's protection.

C.T. expected to at least find human remains in some of the cars, because he had seen men sitting in them, watching the smoke from the *Grandcamp* when he left for his office. It was in one of the cars that he and his team found Elizabeth Dalehite. She was the only living person they found.

Elizabeth Dalehite was the wife of Captain Henry G. Dalehite. She had been watching the fire from their car as her husband walked to the dock area. He was a shipping executive, in charge of assigning port pilots to ships, who just happened to be in Texas City at the time. He did not survive the blast.

When the ship blew up, her car was flattened, and she was badly injured. C.T. and his team found her alive. She was severely wounded and burned. C.T. recognized her but could not remember her first name. As she was being carried out of the fire zone, C.T. quoted scripture to her, saying, "Yea; tho' I walk through the valley of the shadow of death, I will fear no evil."

He said it as much for himself and his team's benefit as for her. He later commented, "Through it all, it was my faith in our loving God that kept me going."

The cars were mostly empty of human remains. All biological tissue, including bones, near to the explosion had apparently been vaporized. All of the cars on the front rows were smashed completely flat, and there were no human remains in any of them.

Cars with blown out windows. Used by permission from the Houston Chronicle.

C.T. had been hoping that people had gotten away. There was nothing to find in the Monsanto employee parking lot because there was nothing left of the men and women who had been sitting in the cars. W. H. Sandberg found a path to the partially destroyed docks and directed C.T. to it on his next trip into the fires.

He continued his rescue efforts until the 4:30 p.m. quitting-time whistle blew at Republic. He then took a five-minute break to rest. He was numb. When asked what it was like in the area, he replied, "Until today I did not know that aluminum could burn. I can guarantee you that it *will* burn and that it *does* burn under certain conditions. Most things will burn."

C.T. had lost count of the number of trips he had made from Sandberg's impromptu marshalling area into the inferno and back. His T-shirt was now stained coal-tar black. Meanwhile, in Galveston, a misting rain of oily smoke began to drape over almost every building in town.

He heard Republic's work whistle over the noise of the fires and continuing explosions. It was comforting to hear it, because he knew that meant that everything was probably under control at Republic.

No one, including C.T., took it as a signal to quit, but in two hours something ominous was about to stop their efforts. He had no idea that he was staggering from place to place. It was growing dark, and the sky had become completely overcast.

Records later showed that the *SS Grandcamp* had loaded 2,300 long tons (5,060,000 pounds) of 32.5%-to-38% ammonium nitrate fertilizer. By comparison, it should be noted that the Oklahoma City bombing of the Murrah Federal Building only used 7,000 lbs. (a little more than 3 long tons) of similar fertilizer, mixed with a little diesel oil in three of the seven barrels. The Oklahoma City fertilizer was not under pressure and nor was it molten.

The initial explosion in Texas City was about 700-times more powerful than the Oklahoma City explosion. Much of the cargo was below the water line, meaning that it could only blow up and out, through the ship's upper hull.

The initial Texas City Disaster explosion remains the strongest non-nuclear explosion ever experienced by mankind at approximately 3 kilotons of explosive force. This is just the initial explosion of the *SS Grandcamp* and not including any of the subsequent explosions, including the *SS High Flyer*. In comparison, Oklahoma City bombing topped out at 0.02 kilotons of explosive force. The tragic wartime explosion in Halifax harbor in 1917 was 2.9 kilotons. The 2020 industrial explosion in Beirut was 1.5 kilotons. To add perspective, the largest conventional explosive employed by any military, the GBU-43 MOAB only has a blast yield of 0.011 kilotons. It would take approximately 273 of these bombs to produce the same blast yield. The United States has only produced twenty GBU-43's. It is important to note that these comparisons are strictly related to blast force and not death toll for each event.

All C.T. knew was that 'disaster' was the mildest word to describe it. It is correct to say that it was the last great explosion related to World War II, as the fertilizer was intended to help rebuild France. Only Hiroshima and Nagasaki had greater explosive power.

Many still see the disaster as having been caused by the local petroleum industry. But that is not true; the explosion was not related to anything manufactured in Texas City.

What caused the explosion was disregard for the rules for shipping ammonium nitrate fertilizer and the use of flammables on the ship. The fact that the fertilizer had been classified by the American Society of Chemical Engineers as non-explosive also contributed to the event.

Certainly, Captain De Guillebon of the *Grandcamp* did not know that he was trying to extinguish an oxidizing explosive, though he was legally required to know the exact nature of his cargo and any possible risks. No one else, including the Texas City Fire Department, even knew that they were fighting a fire fueled by a highly potent oxidizer.

For the citizens of Texas City, it was an overwhelming shock. Many people ran from their homes and places of employment and turned toward the billowing clouds of black smoke. Some dodged falling white-hot steel and rolls of burning sisal. Most were shocked into total silence for a brief time.

Galvestonians also turned their eyes to the north to see the billowing smoke from what appeared to them to be the total destruction of Texas City. Some of them prepared to help, but the closest were fifteen or more miles away, across a lift bridge. The water that separated Texas City from Galveston was only about 2 miles cross. The actual travel distance was formidable.

A few years before the Texas City disaster in 1937, a school building, in New London, Texas had blown up from a natural gas leak. Some Texas City residents initially thought that a New London-type natural gas school explosion had happened to their high school, as the main school complex of high school, junior high, and an elementary school, were only five blocks from the Monsanto plant.

It did not take long for everyone to realize that it was a petrochemical disaster, as secondary explosions continued. No school boiler explosion could have set fires as far away as Carbide and Carbon's[2] plant.

The next few months of their lives were consumed with firefighting, rescue and recovery operations, funerals, and memorials. The last fire was not put out for more than a month.

It had been over eleven hours since the initial explosion when C.T. made it back home to his family. The fires at Republic were under control and this was the first time he found out how his wife and sons had fared; and the first time they had any word of him.

---

[2] Carbide and Carbon is now known as Union Carbide.

8

**Texas City Schools
Weathering the Explosion**

Two of C.T.'s sons, Wally and Nick, had been in class in the elementary school nearest the explosion when it blew up. Their school buildings were badly damaged, but their solid masonry-brick-veneer walls withstood the blast. All windows were blown out, and many doors were jammed by the concussion. Most school buildings shifted on their concrete foundations because of the concussion and were later demolished.

Wally was in the second grade and his class had just taken their seats after saying the pledges to the flags of the United States and Texas. His teacher was asking them to turn in their homework assignments. Wally was relieved that he had not forgotten his work at home.

At the schools, the concussion came simultaneously through the ground and the air. The six-foot tall windows blew in, and glass filled the air before falling all over the room. Wally was knocked out of his desk and got up a little dazed.

Their teacher was also knocked down, but she got up and checked each of the 28 children. All were safe except for a few small cuts. She ran to the door, and it was jammed shut. She tried to open it several times. She even broke off a pair of large scissors she kept in her desk, while trying to pry it open.

Wally's classroom door was among many doors that were jammed in the elementary school building. However, the building had large transoms[1] above each interior door. They had been open in her classroom and remained so.

Wally and his 27 class mates climbed out over the 7' tall transom. His teacher, a small woman, boosted each child up to the transom. No one attempted to climb out the shattered windows, because of the broken glass, the smoke outside, and the sound of continuing explosions.

During the hurried process, Wally fell and broke both the radius and the ulna in his right forearm. His forearm hung down at a 90-degree angle when he held it out from his body. While the bones did not completely pierce his flesh, the pain was excruciating. Wally slumped on the floor in the hall and held his arm out in front of him with the other arm and hand.

The fact that there had been no fire alarm drills may have saved many lives, as most of the students only had to deal with cuts and bruises. All

---

[1] A transom is a window above the door.

windows in the school building facing the explosion had been blown out. If they had been outside on the open play ground, as they would have been during a fire alarm drill, many children might have died instantly from concussion.

Nick, Wally's fourth-grade brother, found Wally lying on the hallway floor outside his class room, clutching his broken arm and screaming. Wally's teacher was nowhere in sight. She was trapped in the room by the jammed door.

Nick tried to reassure Wally and helped him to his feet, helping him cradle his broken forearm. As they made their way out of the elementary school building, most of the people around them were also dazed. Nick looked around at the chaos and the spreading conflagration less than two blocks away and wisely decided to head home.

Nick yelled at the dazed younger students, "Go home! Go home right now!" That galvanized the children into action. Scores of children made their way up the broad street. Out Texas Avenue they poured; some bleeding, many limping, but all headed away from the fires and explosions, toward their homes. Along the way, Nick and Wally said almost nothing to each other, but Nick was very concerned for Wally's arm. It was swelling and turning purple at the fracture site. Nick continually looked around for something to make a splint, but there was nothing. He kept telling Wally, "Hang on! Mom will know what to do!"

And so, they began the 1.5 mile walk back to their house, with Wally holding his dangling broken forearm by the right elbow, in front of him. At first, they tried to run, but Wally screamed with pain after the first step. They had to walk very slowly to keep the forearm from swinging. Over 700 children were streaming away from the school complex. Every step was an agony for Wally but not as bad as it had been to try to run. The initial shock had worn off; his right arm continued to swell both above and below the fracture site.

At 9:12, Nick and Wally's little brother Mike had still been asleep in his bed. He was a very active child, and his mother did not mind him sleeping a little late. Marjorie, their mother, was washing breakfast dishes in the kitchen of their small house. At the age of 4, Mike only knew that something ferocious had fiercely shaken his bed, waking him up.

Mike was extremely annoyed, quickly sat half-way up, looked around, and immediately lay back down. He yanked the heavy chenille bedspread over his head as he lay down, in order to block out the brilliant sunlight. Mike had felt the concussion through the ground. He intended to go back to sleep. As soon as he covered his head, less than a second later, it arrived through the air. The window next to Mike's bed blew in with such great force that shards of glass stuck in the sheetrock wall, six feet away. Tiny glass shards liberally littered his floor, and his bedspread was shredded. But Mike was unhurt. He had no idea what had happened or how important his ducking under the bedspread had proved to be.

Mike very carefully got out of his single bed and in his white Jockey underwear tiptoed very carefully through the broken glass. He ran out the front door, and found his mother in the street, where white-hot steel had just rained down.

One piece of steel, about the size of a football had fallen in the concrete street and Mike peered down at it, still white-hot-with-red-edges and smoldering. He was curiously amazed. That eight by five-inch shard of *SS Grandcamp* had torn its way completely through the four-inch concrete of the street; it was smoldering at the bottom of the crater it had created. It was a solid chunk of steel, thicker than a hull plate.

Mike was so excited that he was not aware of being unclothed and it was unusual that neither of them seemed to notice that he only had on his underpants. His mom never let her boys run around in just their diapers or underpants.

Mom immediately grabbed Mike, ignoring her own clothing rules, and jumped into the 1938 family Dodge four-door, racing toward the school complex, expecting to find the schools blown up. When she was a block away from the school, they met Nick and Wally, walking home.

She saw them from a distance and maneuvered to the curb through the traffic streaming to the school complex. She stopped with a squeal of rubber and jumped out to run to her sons, leaving Mike watching from the car.

Since Wally's arm was obviously broken, his mom looked around for medical help. No help appeared to be available. Long lines had already formed at the Danforth Clinic, one block away. The Danforth Clinic was the only medical facility in town. With over 2000 people seriously injured; all medical services still operable were vastly overwhelmed.

She yelled at the people streaming by her on the sidewalk, "Does anyone know first aid? My little boy has a badly broken arm."

A man walked up and explained that he was an ex-serviceman who knew first aid. He splinted Wally's arm with some slats from a broken fruit crate. They tore up Wally's cotton shirt to make a sling.

Arriving home, the only pain killer Marjorie had was aspirin. She did not know how much she ought to give an eight-year-old; so, she just gave him what she thought was a lot of aspirin for his size. Perhaps not the best choice of the day.

The family took shelter back at home and eventually began to hear the sound of sirens from distant ambulances and fire trucks arriving in Texas City. Help was on its way, but most major help would not reach Texas City for another day. The city was going to be pretty much on its own for the night.

Marjorie quietly talked and prayed with the other women in the Snug Harbor neighborhood where they lived, waiting for news of their husbands. Snug Harbor was its name and it was, for a while that day, a real harbor for some destitute women.

Mike remembers her sitting quietly with about ten other women, in a circle, in chairs, outdoors. It was a small thing, but they were all thankful that it was not yet mosquito season. Every now and then a new explosion would rock them. None of them heard any news of their husbands until after dark that day. Some of them never saw their husbands again.

Marjorie asked them if they knew Jesus as their Savior and Lord. Most said "Yes", two did not answer and one of them said, "No. How do I do that?" Marjorie quoted John 3:16 and 17 to her. "The Bible says, 'For God so loved the world that he gave his only begotten son, that whosoever believeth in him shall never perish, but have everlasting life.' It says that in John 3:16. 3:17 adds, 'For God did not send his Son to condemn the world, but that the world, through him, might be saved.'"

"In Romans, the Bible also tells us to confess with our mouths and believe in our hearts that Jesus is Lord, and that God has raised him from the dead, and we will be saved. Would you like to ask Jesus to save you?"

The lady said, "Yes" and Marjorie quietly led her in a prayer of confession of sin and receiving Jesus as her Savior and Lord. It was to be one of many times in her life that Marjorie led other women to faith in Jesus as their Savior and Lord.

In the house across the street, the wife found the muddy boots of her husband, Jim, in the living room around 8:00 p.m. and wondered if he had come home and gone back to fight fires. To this day, no one knows if Jim was in his automobile in the Monsanto parking lot, came home before the explosion for some reason, or simply ran away after the explosion. Jim was eventually listed among the missing and presumed dead. It is assumed that he was vaporized.

Women would join and leave the group, intermittently. A sociologist would have found it an interesting study as the women almost seemed to take turns breaking down, while others comforted them. A woman who was weeping one minute might be dry-eyed and consoling a neighbor a few minutes later. Several of the women became believers in Jesus Christ.

At four years old, Mike observed how women comfort each other in a shared crisis. He decided, later, as a pastor, that women often take turns grieving and comforting in shared tragedy.

The many flares at the plants usually burned off excess chemical gasses. The reason a lot of gas flared off was because it was poisonous. There was a very real threat that poisonous gas was about to be released by the raging chemical fires. The gas might not burn and would creep through the streets of Texas City if it escaped. One of the worst possible leaks would have been hydrofluoric acid vapor, which was used in making high octane fuel at Republic.

Hydrofluoric acid vapors hug the ground and flow like water. If hydrofluoric acid vapors had been released, it would have killed thousands. There is no doubt about that.

In addition, by 6:30 pm, the *SS High Flyer* had begun burning and was thought to be close to explosion; no one knew how the fire propagated on *High Flyer*. Efforts would be made, in the flame-lit night, to tow the powerless ship out into Galveston Bay, where it was hoped that any explosion would dissipate over the open waters.

High Flyer had not been under any power at the time of the explosion. With her steam turbine broken down for maintenance, and the engine's 25-thousand-pound turbine cover lying on her deck, she was powerless on April 16th. She was not only a dead ship; she was about to become a vaporized ship.

C.T. went home to take his family to safety. It was dark and the only light came from the fires. The low-hanging black smoke made it difficult to see any distance at all. Heavy clouds hung over the city. Whether they were smoke or clouds enhanced by smoke is not known.

Around 10:00 PM, someone realized that the giant searchlights supporting the naval guns installed at Fort Stewart, on Galveston, could be trained on Texas City, instead of just out to sea into the Gulf of Mexico. They could light the sea for over twelve miles. For many nights after the 16th, they were trained on specific sites in Texas City to aid in firefighting and rescue efforts. The first such site was the burning *SS High Flyer*.

The searchlights had been installed with the giant multi-inch naval cannons on the island, before or during the war, to help fight any enemy ships that might appear. As it happened, the guns were never fired in combat, and the greatest service of the searchlights was to be in illuminating parts of Texas City's chemical facilities during the continuing efforts to save the city. They were trained on the *High Flyer* and the *Keene*.

Because Marjorie had the lone family car, C.T. had to walk the 1.5 miles to their house. When he came to the house, the power was off, and the entire street was dark. The now cloudy sky, filled by smoke and natural clouds, was pulsating red as it reflected the thousands of fires, large and small. It looked like a living thing, expanding and boiling above the city.

C.T. wearily stepped on the porch and opened the screen door, saying, "Don't be afraid, it's me." Marjorie heard him and screamed, 'Tommy!' They embraced, both weeping.

He had been completely misted with crude oil and he smelled of smoke, blood, sulfur, human remains, and unknown chemicals. He looked absolutely dreadful.

His gold-rim glasses were broken at the right earpiece and held together with a piece of filthy string. His fedora hat was not to be seen and his hair was scruffy, oil saturated, and unruly. After he assured her that he was okay, he listened to her story. It was only then that the family learned how the whole thing had begun.

He told them it was a ship named the *SS Grandcamp* and that he had been onboard that ship only fifteen minutes before the explosion. He told them how the plant manager at Republic Oil had released him to go back to the office and that the manager and other men from his office must all be dead. They quietly rejoiced and cried, overwhelmed with both joy and sadness.

Mike ate his peanut butter and grape jelly sandwich and did not pay much attention to what his Dad was saying. Marjorie expressed her guilt at being among the living in a silent prayer to God. She was a very religious woman and always felt guilt when someone died, and she was still alive.

C.T. told them of the immediate poison gas scare. He washed up as best he could but was unable to shower because of low water pressure throughout the city. He hated that he could not wash his hair and only barely had enough water to shave. However, C.T. did not complain out loud, as he knew that except for an amazing act of providence, he would not be alive.

Marjorie packed very few clothes in one small suitcase, making sure she had aspirin for Wally, and they hastily left town, heading up the road on the west side of Galveston Bay, Texas Highway 146. They were thankful that war rationing was over and that they would be able to refill the car if they needed to.

Wally came along of course; having not seen any physician after the veteran had splinted his arm. His mom gave him two aspirin every four hours and hoped that she was not poisoning him. Nick was silent; and Mike prattled about everything he saw along the way, seemingly oblivious to the moment's importance.

C.T. did not show much agitation as he drove. However, he customarily drove with his right hand at the top of the steering wheel, occasionally flicking his two middle fingers against his thumb every now and then. That night he flicked those fingers on his thumb continuously.

After dark that night, most of the residents of Texas City also left town if they could. Some went to Galveston, but most headed north or west. Emergency relief from Galveston, Houston, and even as far away as Los Angeles, California, began to head for Texas City. Eventually, over 200 firemen would be on scene. Most were men experienced in fighting chemical fires, including the Los Angeles contingent.

The first motel with available rooms was a small wooden structure of ten-or-so rooms in Dayton, Texas. There was one room with two double beds still available. They checked in about 10:30 pm. C.T. took a welcomed shower and they tried to sleep.

Wally finally fell asleep around 11:00 pm, in spite of his increasing pain. Four-year-old Mike was exhausted and fell asleep as soon as he lay down. The sky, to the south of them, continued to pulse with red, orange, and purple colors. C.T. took one last look, shook his head, and muttered under his breath, "So many dead! So very many dead!" Then he shut the screen door to their room, latched it, and shut and locked the outer door.

Mom reminded each of them to say their prayers. Mike remembers whispering; "Now I lay me down to sleep. I pray the Lord my soul to keep. If I should die before I wake... (Pause)." He then thought about what he was praying and realized that he could have died that day. It was the first time in his young life that he ever seriously thought about death. He finished very fervently, "... I pray the Lord my soul to take."

Mike was not aware of his soul; but he already knew that if his soul was to go anywhere someday, he wanted it to go to God. Sometime after midnight, as Mike remembers it, the entire room shook and the screen door on the room banged like it was being hit with a fast fuselage of fists. It was the second time that Mike had been awakened by a shaking bed. He was annoyed again, but also highly curious.

C.T. yelled out at the top of his strong voice, "Who is it?" But it was no one, of course. He went outside and saw the fresh fires blooming over Texas City. Texas City was around 45 miles south of Dayton, but it still lit the skies over Dayton quite brightly. C.T. could see his distinct shadow against the white clapboard motel building.

9

SS High Flyer

April 17, 1945

12:55 am

AFTER THE FIRST EXPLOSION, THE *SS High Flyer* had shown external damage, but she was still afloat and not burning. She and the *Keene* became the responsibility of the Coast Guard to remove from the vicinity. Since neither ship was burning around noon on the 16th, it was decided to leave them in place as other fires were fought and recovery work progressed.

The nearest Coast Guard base and lifeboat station was on the northeast side of Galveston, next to the Bolivar-to-Galveston ferry landing. Since the war, her lone cutter had been repositioned and the main functions of the base were open ocean rescue, customs enforcement, maritime law enforcement, and buoy maintenance.

The radioman on duty at the time of the initial *Grandcamp* explosion felt it through his chair before he heard it. He immediately ran outside and saw the rising fire and smoke in Texas City. Then, he saw the water at the piers where the Coast Guard vessels were moored rise over three feet. Only one of the mooring hawsers broke, so the vessels were not damaged. He immediately called his commanding officer's residence at Fort Stewart and was informed that the Commander was on his way and to stand by.

As explosions and new fires raged in Texas City, a decision was made after a telephone conference with Lykes Lines in New Orleans, to tow the *High Flyer* out to Galveston Bay. It was felt the *Wilson B Keene* and its partially loaded cargo of wheat flour was not a significant danger.

This required tug boats. At 9:50 am, G & H towing company got a phone call from the Coast Guard requesting two tugs to tow *High Flyer* away. G&H dispatched *Albatross* and *Propeller*. When those tugs arrived at 10:50 am, they found they could not enter the harbor.

Their captains noticed survivors on the earthen banks left from dredging the harbor and removed them from those spoiled banks. Some of the survivors were not badly injured, while others were severely injured and/or burned.

Both tugs returned to Galveston with their survivors and Texas City was left without any tugs to tow the *High Flyer*. SS *High Flyer* was not noticed to be burning. She was resting side-by-side to the *Keene* and still anchored by her bow.

The combination of burning sulfur, burning chemicals, and other heavy smoke sources caused both remaining ships to be evacuated. It was assumed that the *Keene* could not be moved, because her engine room was filled with steam from her own ruptured boilers.

High Flyer and *Keene* sat, moored, in the middle of fires and explosions for the rest of the day and into the night of April 16. No flames were observed on their decks and initially no smoke was seen rising from their superstructures.

At 6:30 p.m. smoke was first seen rising from *High Flyer*'s sealed hatches. It has never been determined how the fire spread to the inside of *High Flyer*'s hold #3. The conjecture at the time was that her hull was heated by the nearby flames and that something spontaneously combusted within her hold.

It was then that J.G. Tompkins of Lykes Brothers Steamship Company became involved. Both *Wilson B. Keene* and *SS High Flyer* belonged to his company, and he wanted to save them, even if only for salvage.

It was 8:00 p.m. on the 16th when Tompkins called the President of G & H towing and requested four tugs, four crews, oxy-acetylene torches and crews, gas masks, and other equipment. He had great difficulty convincing G & H representatives that they should make the attempts to tow *High Flyer* and *Keene*.

There were at least six phone calls between New Orleans and Galveston. In the meantime, the smoke on *High Flyer* changed from grayish white to orange, indicating that the fire had spread to the FGAN onboard.

SS Wilson B Keene continued to show no signs of fire. It had already been decided that *Keene* could not be moved until *High Flyer* was removed. J. G. Tompkins had demanded four tugs because he knew that it would take two tugs for each of the vessels. The six very stressful phone calls with G & H Towing covered two subjects, the hesitancy of crews to go without a large bonus and a 50% recovery fee to G & H for each ship and cargo saved.

Even the minimum fee for unsuccessful attempts seemed outrageous to Lykes Brothers Vice-President Tompkins. He finally agreed to $100,000 for the deployment of the four tugs, successful or not.

Finally, at 10:15 pm, the first tug left Galveston. Forty-five minutes later, it arrived at the Texas City basin. The last of the four tugs arrived at 11:20 pm. By this time, *SS High Flyer* had only 105 minutes, or so, to exist. An hour and forty-five minutes may seem like a long time, but if one has to maneuver tugs, attach lines, burn away anchor chains, etc., it is not very ample.

Albatross and *Propeller* took two hawsers and attached them to the anchor chain on *High Flyer* and began to pull. Their engines were run to maximum RPM. Nothing happened. The tow line stretched, and the sterns of the tugs were actually below water level, but nothing moved. *SS High Flyer* did not budge. Suddenly, both tow hawsers broke. The sound could be heard by those on shore even over the hissing roar of petroleum fires.

By this time, 12:05 am, smoke of various colors was pouring from hatches 2, 3, and 4. The smoke from hatch #4 was bright orange. By now, everyone knew that meant that the FGAN was burning.

Three of the tugs backed out of the basin and stood by while another attempt was made to attach a ten-inch hawser. The tug *J. R. Guyton* already had a large hawser rigged onboard, so she moved into position and had just attached the hawser when orders came from Coast Guard headquarters in Galveston to evacuate the area.

J.R. Guyton was the last to pull away, leaving her valuable hawser attached to *High Flyer*. She stopped at the mouth of the basin, to watch what would happen. She was prepared to return and try to pull out the *Keene* if the *High Flyer* exploded. Nothing happened for a few minutes. Then, at approximately 1:05 am, *High Flyer* lived up to her name by exploding. *High Flyer* was obliterated by the explosion of 960 long tons of molten FGAN and over 2,000 tons of sulfur.

Keene had her stern-half torn away and destroyed while her bow simply sank. On board the *Guyton*, one man was severely wounded by flying shrapnel and the tug was made inoperable. She was down by the bow, listing 5 degrees and her engines would not restart.

Albatross and *Propeller* took pumps aboard *Guyton*, managed to stop most of the leaking in her forward hull, and towed her to Galveston.

High Flyer's explosion resulted in similar damage to that of the *Grandcamp*. In effect, the Texas City Docks no longer existed, and many more fires started in the adjacent plants. The bravery of the men on the tugs cannot be over-stated.

The front half of *Keene* would not be salvaged for several months. The explosion that completed the sinking and final destruction of the *Keene*, also added to the overall carnage, and was almost as large as the initial explosion. Many more secondary fires were started in the petrochemical complex of Texas City.

The 25,000-pound turbine engine cover flew through the air to Republic's west side and fell on a pump building. It completely flattened the building and put those pumps out of action. Republic had some men hurt, but no one was killed.

George McCrocklin was still at the refinery. He stood with his hands on his hips, looking at the destroyed pump shed. He turned to the man next to him and said, "I guess we had better go to plan B for routing liquids. This route is completely lost to us." George sighed and went back to the E&I shack.

Fortunately, due to the poison gas/explosion scare, most people were away from the area when the *High Flyer* blew up, and only one death occurred; however, another 100 brave men were injured.

It was the 960 long-tons (2,112,000 pounds) of ammonium nitrate aboard the *SS High Flyer* that exploded. The attempt to tow *High Flyer* out to Galveston Bay kept failing due to wreckage in the harbor snagging the ship. Finally, the tugs were withdrawn back to Galveston; by 1:50 am, most of the area was evacuated and allowed to burn for the night.

The Fort Stewart spotlights, which could illuminate Galveston Bay almost all the way to the mouth of the Trinity River near Houston, were also shut down. Their weary crews went home with the notice that they needed to be back on duty by dark on the 17th.

SS High Flyer was totally destroyed and mostly vaporized like the *Grandcamp*. The inclusion of a large amount of sulfur in her holds increased the overall effect and threw molten, burning sulfur all over the area. The smoke from the sulfur combined with the humidity of the night air produced diluted sulfuric acid. Many of the burns that night came from sulfuric acid-laced smoke.

High Flyer's cargo also included disassembled wooden rail cars for the decimated French railway system. Parts of the cars flew through the air, burning furiously. Including the two ships' cargoes, the debris from the two explosions now covered more than a 7,000-foot diameter semi-circle in Texas City.

Parts of *High Flyer* fell into the residential areas. Most of the ships' parts were white hot upon landing. It remains a mystery why a city-wide fire did not consume the town.

10

The Day After

April 17, 1945

Daytime

WHEN THE POISON GAS SCARE was over, early on the 17th, the family returned home. That morning, they found a café in Dayton and ate a somber breakfast. The bacon, sunny-side-up eggs and toast tasted good to Mike, but Wally was not hungry, and C.T. acted like his food was almost alien in origin. When they found out the family was from Texas City, the café management gave them their breakfasts free of charge.

It was to be four days before Wally would see a physician in La Marque. On the twentieth of April, Wally's arm was re-set properly, without surgery. He had to wait until the more seriously injured were treated. Doctor Weldon G. Kolb was not sure if it would heal properly after waiting four days to be properly set, but it did.

The family that lived immediately across the street from C.T.'s family lost their father Jim, as he had worked at the styrene facility at Monsanto.

Like many men, and even quite a few women, he simply went to work on April 16 and was not seen again after C.T. talked to him. His muddy work boots had been found in his living room after dark on the 16th, but he did not return home. Whether he came home and went back to fight the fires or came home and just ran away has never been proved.

With the open windows and the proximity of the small houses, people knew that there had been loud disagreements between Jim and his wife. C.T. and Marjorie thought he might have run away if he wasn't killed outright. However, it is most likely the boots were already in his house, and he never came home.

Jim became one of the over 180 or more people that were ultimately listed as missing and presumed dead. Every male office worker at Republic Refining other than C.T. was also on that list. Most of the dayshift at Monsanto Chemical were killed, while others were severely injured. The most common injuries were burns, soft-tissue concussion damage, and broken bones.

Almost every type of injury a man might have suffered in combat in WWII was experienced in Texas City. No bullet wounds were recorded, but there were many small flying missiles that produced similar injuries. Shrapnel injuries were very common.

It will never be known how many seamen were killed; nor were the names of most stevedores discovered. In reality, the total death loss remains an undiscoverable number. 600 dead is not an unreasonable estimate.

11

The Gymnasium-Morgue

Texas City and Galveston

April 17, 1945

C.T.'s ARDUOUS WORK HAD ONLY begun. With the arrival of fire fighters from around the country, C.T. was assigned to rescue and body recovery. While rescue attempts lasted only two days, the recovery of human remains went on for months.

In the beginning, the county coroner was overwhelmed. Most of the recognizable bodies were taken to John Sealy Hospital in Galveston, where several coroners combined their efforts. John Sealy also had more refrigeration capacity than any other facility nearby. It was and is a teaching hospital of the University of Texas Medical School system.

Refrigeration facilities at the port of Galveston for the fishing industry were also used for a while. No one ever knew in coming years that the shrimp they were eating had been refrigerated in the same facilities as bodies had been stored.

John Sealy received most of the injuries in the first three days. The University of Texas Medical School at John Sealy Hospital provided barely enough physicians to handle the patient load of wounds, broken bones, and especially burns.

Many medical students got their first taste of trauma cases. It became a positive mark on each person's resume' that they had participated in trauma treatment at Galveston after Texas City. However, some of the young doctors and interns decided that they would never go near a trauma room again.

There were no ambulances or hearses in Texas City, so C.T. helped remove the seats from the four donated Galveston city buses and then helped load the buses with possibly recognizable corpses for Galveston. Less identifiable bodies remained in Texas City. With over 580 missing or presumed dead, the task was enormous. The problem that arose was that there were so many unrecognizable bodies, and an incredible number of body parts.

As the only living executive employee from his refinery, C.T. also managed and represented the Republic Oil refinery until a new plant manager could be on-site. He split his time between refinery concerns and the morgue set up at the Texas City High School gym. He worked at the gym-morgue during the day and at the refinery in the evenings.

The initial morgue was set up in a local Buick dealership showroom, but it was quickly overwhelmed with bodies. C.T. helped transport the first bus load of human remains to the high school gymnasium, where he helped lay them out on the floor.

A Roman Catholic priest from the Archdiocese of Galveston-Houston came in, beginning at the dealership, and later at the morgue, and gave last rights to each body. Two local Roman Catholic priests eventually shared the duty of providing last rights for all bodies; since they did not know who was Roman Catholic and who was not.

Soon the doors of the gymnasium/morgue were opened for survivors to look for their lost loved ones. Only one person from each family was allowed to search at a time.

C.T. spent several days after his return from Dayton, guiding people through the facility. The remains were first laid out haphazardly on the floor, under tarps and blankets. After a few days, the effort became more organized, and the remains were put in orderly rows, with corresponding numbers on the remains, the tarps and the blankets.

The gymnasium/morgue. Used by permission from the Houston Chronicle.

The U.S. Army Reserve unit in Galveston provided the tarps and blankets as palls. If they became too soaked with blood, they were replaced with new ones; and the soiled palls were burned in Galveston. No new fires were lit in Texas City, even to burn medical waste.

People desperately looking for their lost loved ones were escorted through, one or two adult family members at a time; and each pall was lifted to let them view the remains underneath. In some cases, the only thing left covered by the pall was a lower torso and legs, if they still existed.

This was C.T.'s task. He was in charge of the four escorts on duty. He would lead people through the aisles of remains, lifting each tarp or blanket, in reluctant hope that all the bodies would eventually be identified.

After each trip through, C.T. hurried to the boys' shower room and threw up, washed his face and combed his hair with his black Ace brand Bakelite comb, and returned to the main floor of the gym, ready to escort someone else through the macabre scene. His revulsion and resultant nausea at the smells and sights of burned bodies and burst bowels did not deter him from his duty.

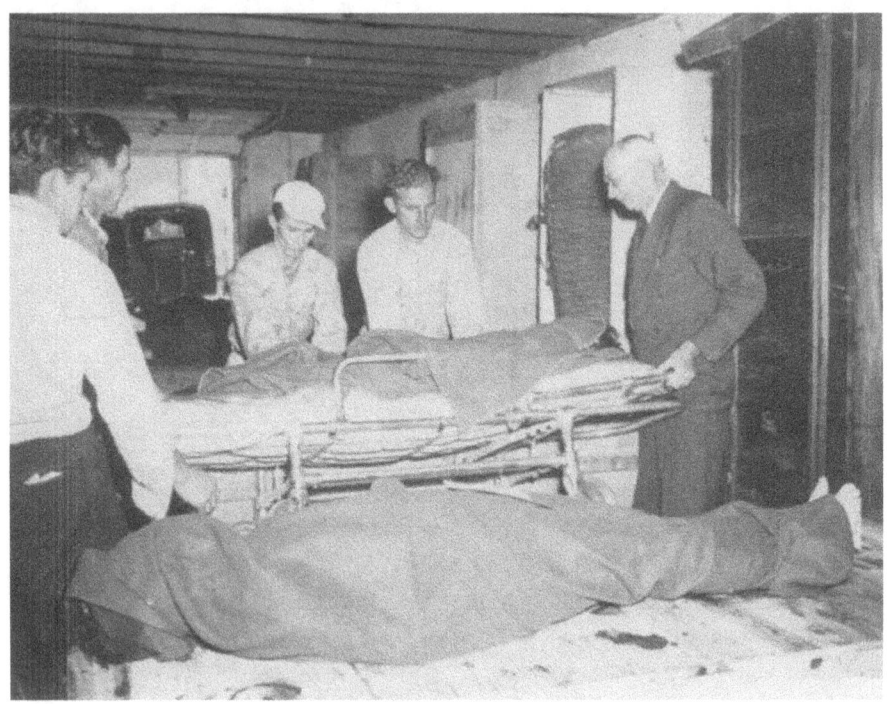

One of several makeshift morgues used after the disaster.
Used by permission from the University of North Texas library system.

Some people came through the morgue more than once, over several days, as new remains arrived. C.T. could only imagine the hope and the fear in each survivor's mind. Some of them, on their second or third trip, would specifically ask for C.T. to guide them, as they had learned how gentle and compassionate he was. He always remembered them and greeted them by name when they came to the gym for a second or third time. C.T. always prayed with them, both before they went in, and after each tarp was lifted. He hoped his prayers comforted them as much as they did him.

If people he had known before the disaster, were in line, C.T. would ask the Red Cross representative to allow him to be their escort. His request was always granted.

Since there would be possible confusion due to the emotional state of the survivors, identification by two family members or friends became the rule. It was a slow process, and C.T. was able to make his vomitorium trips between the escorts he provided.

Eventually the morgue in the high school gym was closed, due to the decomposition of the bodies. C.T.'s last task in body recovery was supervising the loading of those few decomposing remains in Texas City on the stripped buses for removal to the expanded morgue at John Sealy, for further identification efforts.

Families of victims wait outside the gymnasium/morgue for a chance to identify their loved ones. Used by permission from the Houston Chronicle.

C.T.'s most vivid memory of those four days was when there were around fifty bodies under tarps and blankets. He escorted a young widow through the gym. She viewed each set of remains very carefully and said, "No. That is not my husband," each time. Her voice was soft and tremulous. She explained to C.T. that they had been married only three months and her husband had taken the good paying job in Texas City. Their married life was only just beginning. After viewing all the bodies and assorted body parts, C.T. led her to the exit. She was weeping inconsolably because she still did not know her husband's fate. All she knew was that he was missing.

As C.T. turned to go to the 'vomitorium', she stopped weeping, stood up straight, very erect, paused, and asked in a firm voice, "Sir, may I look at one body again; or am I only allowed to look once?" C.T. said, "Of course we can go back. Which of the tarps are you interested in?" She pointed to a tarp-covered set of remains, number 26. C.T. knew that body well. It was badly burned and cut up on the upper torso. It had been the cause of several of his trips to the washroom to vomit.

He led the young widow, supporting her by her left arm, back to the very middle of the rows of tarp-covered bodies and she asked him to lift the pall from the horribly mangled remains. The body's legs and feet were still covered after he lifted the tarp. The torso and head remains were unrecognizable to her from blast and burns. She shuddered and C.T. thought she might faint, but she only swayed a little. She then asked C.T., "Are you allowed to uncover his feet?" C.T. did not answer; but gently replaced the pall on the torso and head. He then completely removed the tarp from the legs and feet.

Remarkably, the legs and feet were unblemished except for the bluish color of death. The shoes were gone. C.T. knew that a victim's shoes were not removed for the identifications because they sometimes provide what was needed by the survivors to make the identification. The victims shoes had been blown off.

It was then that the young widow's unusual reason for the request to see the legs and feet became clear. The young widow stood staring at the undamaged bare feet, fell to her knees on the basketball court's wooden floor, and cried out, "Those are my husband's feet! Those are *his* feet! Those are *his* feet!"

Two other men heard her cries and came over. The men helped her up, each man holding one of her arms. They gently walked her to the Red Cross' identification table; C.T. went back to cover the feet and put a new label on the body. He never saw her again; he did, however, make another immediate trip to the boys' shower room. He had begun to think of it as the 'vomitorium', as he was not the only man or woman assigned to the gymnasium that frequented it.

The young widow's foot-recognition was accepted as identification by the Red Cross representatives. It helped that the man's feet fit a 13 ½ shoe.

Actually, any type of positive identification was accepted in the gymnasium morgue. The authorities figured it was better to be buried under an incorrect name than under no name at all. Although tender care was taken to assure that identifications were sound, even if any mistaken identifications were made, no one cared a great deal. Jim's body was never identified, if it was there.

Working under such conditions can harden a person's heart. The horror of volunteering in that gym did the opposite to C.T. as it softened his heart to the misery of others. That softening was to such an extent that he became known for the rest of his life for his philanthropic volunteering.

He became a deacon in his future church in La Marque, served as its Treasurer, and became President of the local Lion's Club. In the late 1950's he was named La Marque's Man of the Year and was elected to the La Marque Independent School Board and served until 1962.

C.T. helped steam-clean the gym and set up the Red Cross clothing and food center on the same site after the bodies were removed. After that, most of his time was consumed with talking to Republic employees that were injured or to the families of the dead employees. Within one week, most of the dead union employees no longer received a pay check, and many of the living were out of work until the refinery could be repaired and back on line.

C.T. also helped ten widows file their workers' compensation claims, which in Texas, at that time, were limited to $2500. Those whose husbands were missing, and presumed dead received no compensation for many days, months, and even years.

The styrene plant was never rebuilt and most living Monsanto employees, who normally worked the second and third shifts, also had no work. Many of the survivors simply left town.

Eventually Monsanto built a different chemical facility on their land. The decisions by Monsanto, Republic, and Carbide and Carbon to rebuild saved Texas City as a chemical powerhouse. The Monsanto plant was later sold to Sterling Chemicals in 1986.

The American Red Cross was soon on the scene in force late on the 17th, but there was little they could do in the days immediately following the explosions in Texas City.

However, there was a negative incident that resulted from poor communications. The Red Cross initially sold their donuts to rescue workers for 5¢ apiece, which angered many a Texas City resident.

To their credit, the Red Cross provided free donuts and coffee the next day for the rescue workers. The Red Cross volunteers had thought they were working in a canteen mode and had been used to charging when operating a canteen. C.T. complained to a Red Cross official at the gymnasium, "Do you know that your volunteers outside are selling donuts and coffee?" The obviously shocked official replied, "Are you sure?" He answered, "I am sure without a doubt."

The official replied, "That is unthinkable. I promise you I will set this straight." It was not completely set straight for nearly 4 hours; but it was eventually corrected.

The Red Cross' blood service was not used much because most victims of the disaster were not wounded to the point of large blood loss. The reason relatively little blood was needed was that if you were present for the event, you were either lightly wounded or dead.

However, the citizens of the United States responded with a massive out-pouring of money, clothes, food, and donated blood. All donations were handled efficiently by the Red Cross. After more than two weeks, every fire was put out, and the reconstruction process began. Houses destroyed near the Monsanto property were never rebuilt, and the empty streets are a stark reminder of the disaster to this day.

C.T. saw to it that Republic Oil and Refining Company became fully operational within two weeks, except for four or five large storage tanks that were burned out.

The men at the refinery, including C.T.'s brother George, knew how badly everyone needed work. Ultimately, Texas City was rebuilt, and its petrochemical operations continue in a vastly enlarged way today. Texas City remains a chemical powerhouse of even greater importance than it was in 1947.

Many buried isolated human remains are still assumed to be under the bull-dozed Monsanto site; some isolated bones are found from time-to-time as excavations happen at the current chemical plant. The badly damaged solid bronze propeller from the *SS High Flyer* and an anchor from the *Grandcamp* are displayed in a memorial near the dike.

Republic was eventually sold to Marathon Oil and has been expanded and improved through the intervening decades. The office building from 1947 still stands near the front road by the refinery. If a person stands with his back to the railway and looks a little to the west-north-west, the two-story masonry/brick building C.T. where worked is still there, as part of the Marathon Refinery.

*Memorial Cemetery is where most of the remains are buried.
Used by permission from Melissa Roberts.*

The road that runs in front of Marathon is the one that C.T. used to go to the pier. The rescue center he worked out of was where the railroad and street cross.

Before and after the disaster: Top left is the location of the SS Grandcamp (1), the SS High Flyer (2), and the Wilson B. Keene (3). Top right is during the disaster. Bottom left is just after the disaster, and bottom right is the Port of Texas City today. Used by permission from the Houston Chronicle.

SS High Flyer's solid bronze propeller was found over 700 feet inland from the port and has several pieces missing from it. That site is near the exact location of W. H. Sandberg's first command center. Other than the propeller from *High Flyer and Grandcamp's* anchors in Texas City, both ships only remain as fragments rusting in the waters of the bay.

The Gymnasium-Morgue 89

The propeller of the SS High Flyer. Used by permission from Melissa Roberts.

The anchor of the SS Grandcamp. Used by permission from Melissa Roberts.

12

Federal Court

Houston

1957

THUS, IT WAS LONG AFTER most of the visible scars from the Texas City disaster had healed, that responsibility for the entire event was accepted by both the U.S. and the French governments. That was partially because of the national flags of the two ships involved; and because the fertilizer had been casually manufactured, improperly labeled, and improperly shipped from the US defense munitions plants.

A federal tort case brewed for six years. No one wanted to take responsibility for the explosion. The Federal Courts Tort Act was enacted in 1945 after a U.S. Army Air bomber had flown into the Empire State Building. It was found that the Army was negligent in that air disaster. The Federal Courts Tort Act (FCTA) was enacted by Congress shortly after the plane crash. However, since it was enacted after the plane crash, no court actions could be taken in the New York incident. The FCTA made it possible for citizens to sue the Federal Government for disasters partially caused by federal negligence. The FCTA had been modified in June of 1946, just in time for the Texas City disaster.

The case from over 8,000 claimants was consolidated by the court into Dalehite v: Untied States. That court found in favor of the claimants. However, that decision was later overturned on appeal by the Supreme Court, and of the 8,400-plus claimants in the original Texas City case, only 1,394 eventually received any compensation.

The US Supreme Court had ruled that the only way compensation could be paid was if Congress enacted a payment and the President signed the act. That act of congress, led by Congressman Clark W. Thompson, Dem., Texas, caused some survivors to collect in 1958. The *Dalehite vs. United States* case resulted in the Dalehite estate receiving $49,000 in compensation. It was awarded under the Thompson bill because the family lost their father to the initial explosion and their mother when she succumbed due to burns and injuries she received. Ultimately, most of the claimant money was paid to companies rather than individuals or their estates.

C.T. would get up in La Marque early each day, read the Galveston Daily News, have at least two cups of coffee, and wait for the federal marshal. Before daylight each day, the same marshal would and transport him to Federal Court in Houston. After court, the marshal would return C.T. home to La Marque. The trip took at least 1 ½ hours, each way.

When the US Coast Guard held their formal investigation of the explosions in September of 1947, they had not known that C.T. was the last person alive at the scene, so they did not call him to testify. By 1957, most other survivors from the immediate scene did not have C.T.'s last minute details.

C.T. was almost certain that he would not have to testify about anything because he had not known anything until the day it all happened. He was wrong in that assumption. His testimony became critical to the case.

As the last person known to have left the site alive in 1947, C.T. was an invaluable witness at the 1957 court event. After responsibility for the disaster was established by the court, C.T.'s most important testimony concerned *exactly which people* he personally knew were present at the site when he left it; since so many of them had been vaporized.

Each weekday during the trial in 1957, C.T. would take the stand in Federal Court in Houston and answer probing questions. Commonly, the questions were something like, "Did you see a certain person when you left?" A typical answer by C.T. might be, "Yes. He was standing next to a car, smoking a cigarette with two other men" giving their names, also. Far too often he had to say, "No. I do not recall that person." Very many times, though, he was the sole witness to establish that someone had been present and therefore could be assumed to be deceased.

C.T.'s testimony went on for about four weeks, as he was closely questioned about people still missing and presumed dead. He proved himself to have a remarkable memory, as he was able to describe the exact places, he had seen particular people as he left the disaster site.

The story would not be over until 1959, two years after C.T. became the key witness in the Federal Tort Suit. It was the first tort suit ever to be brought against the US government. His testimony was used solely to prove that those missing and believed dead were actually dead.

The trips to Houston Federal Court continued for at least a month. Vaporization leaves so little remains that even modern-day forensics probably would not have been able to identify some of the dead that C.T. was able to place at the scene.

C.T. never knew how many of the families of people he identified received compensation. He was nevertheless unhappy at the final outcome in 1959, when only 1,394 claims had been paid. Unforeseen loopholes in Congressman Clark Thompson's hastily enacted law left thousands of people and small businesses without standing in the case.

Some of the 1,394 litigants paid were corporations such as Monsanto Chemical and Carbide and Carbon, so the actual payout per victim is hard to trace. Even if all the payouts had been the maximum allowed by law, no person could have received more than $25,000 for a single death. Thus, out of the possible 8,400-plus litigants, the final 1,394 payees received less than $25,000 per death. If the entire 8,400 possible litigants had divided the total award, they would have received an average of a little more than $2,000, each.

It remains true that over 7,000 claimants received no compensation for their financial and physical losses during the Texas City Disaster. The most any one estate received (Dalehite) was $49,000. Because Mrs.

Dalehite suffered from her injuries for several years before she died, her estate was given the largest award.

Sum total, the cost of reconstruction exceeded $117 million in 1950 values. That would make the cost exceed $1.5 billion in today's dollars. All three ships were written off, and their values are not included in the reconstruction costs, since they had been sold for $1 each after the war. Most of the costs for losses and reconstruction were borne by the individuals involved, and the corporations that lost chemical plant facilities.

C.T.'s testimony only helped some of the 1,394 final litigants, but he would have thought the three-plus weeks of testimony well worth his time if *anyone* received compensation. He just did not like it that so many were left out of the compensation pool.

C.T. never tried to make a claim for his hearing loss, as he considered it nothing as compared to the losses of others. Because he was a salaried employee, he did not lose a day's pay. C.T. ran the Republic operations until June of 1947, when a new Plant Manager arrived. C.T. was glad to relinquish the responsibility.

Years of reconstruction followed. Republic was repaired and then expanded as its role moved from only producing aviation grade fuel to also producing many other chemicals. C.T. continued to work there until 1962. Plymouth Oil eventually bought Republic Oil in 1957, while Marathon Oil bought Plymouth Oil in 1962, and the refinery changed names.

When Marathon Oil bought Plymouth Oil, C.T., and most Texas executive employees left the company. C.T. was offered a position with the company in Saudi Arabia but did not accept it as he had an eight-year-old daughter and preferred to raise her in Houston.

C.T. entered the Real Estate business in Houston. In 1973, he was showing a ranch to a prospective buyer near Hempstead, Texas, when he quietly and quickly passed away from a burst aortic aneurysm.

Remembering the people was not all that C.T. was to carry in his mind and heart. For him, the Texas City Disaster was not just what happened on April 16. It was a series of events that remained vivid in his memories until his death in 1973. A few survivors of the disaster attended his funeral at Galveston County Memorial Park Cemetery, in Hitchcock.

13

Flashbacks

Republic Refining Company Offices

Winter, 1947

ON DECEMBER FIRST, 1947, A small ceremony was held at Republic Oil. All employees were invited, except for those essential to plant operational safety. C.T. and a few other men were presented with engraved solid gold, curved-back, Hamilton presentation wrist watches. The engraving on the solid gold back of C.T.'s watch reads as follows:

Presented to
C.T. McCrocklin
For Courageous Action
Texas City Disaster
April 16-17, 1947
Republic Oil Refining Company

C.T. and the men who received the watches said very little. As their chief spokesman, C.T. said, "Thank you very much for this watch. But for the grace of God many more people would have died. I am certainly one of those people. Even though the main cause of the explosion was something not even manufactured in Texas City, her citizens and Republic's employees bore the disastrous result of several errors. As far as courageous action is concerned, all I can say for myself is that when the disaster happened, I just did what had to be done. I am sure that each of these other men would say something similar. Let us hope, pray, and work diligently that nothing like this disaster ever happens again."

His brother George did not get a watch. C.T. thought he should have. After the presentation of the watches, there was white cake and a little fruit punch and coffee served. Then, everyone quickly went back to work, because there was petroleum to be refined. After seventy years, the watch still keeps perfect time.

Texas City, Texas, USA, 2014

The number of living survivors continues to dwindle, and the horrors of the disaster are no longer shared by many people. However, some say that the peculiar, sweet smell of the disaster can still be noticed in downtown Texas City on hot summer days.

The facades of several buildings downtown were made of decorative limestone, sandstone, or brick. They were impregnated with vapor and other particles on those fateful April days in 1947. Although the smells of current refining are still very prevalent in modern Texas City, there is an odor that only 1947 disaster survivors can recognize. It seems to ooze out of the masonry and sandstone buildings downtown, even today. Hot, still weather makes it easier to recognize.

That odor is unique. It is a combination of the sweet odors of exploded ammonium nitrate, of many chemicals, oil, fire, smoke, and also of human death. However, it is not unpleasant. It is just different; and it smells *very* sweet. A person has to have been there in 1947 to recognize it.

For many modern residents, it probably smells to them sort of like Texas City is *supposed* to smell. To the survivors it is a special odor that stirs their memories of disaster and heroics. Like the oil that escapes from the USS Arizona, the FGAN odor may never go away; but time may eventually erase its memory.

The chemical complex in Texas City today is at least twice as large as it was in 1947. The employees go about their daily work fully aware that their city must take special precautions. There have been other smaller explosions and fires at various Texas City facilities since 1947. Although there have been a few fatalities, none of them has been anything near disaster status. The greatest hazard today may be hydrofluoric acid. There are imminent plans to take the hydrofluoric acid out of the refining process for aviation grade gasoline at Marathon.

The smoke stacks, steam whistles, and waste-product flares from the processing are ever-prevalent. They represent a robust economy; the citizens of Texas City and La Marque welcome all that a robust economy means to them.

Texas City boasts one of the finest emergency preparedness plans of any American city. It has a highly trained disaster team. Each chemical plant or refinery trains with the city fire department to fight fires.

Most of the scars of April 1947 are gone. Only cemetery memorials, a few pieces of the original ships on display, museum displays, and three totally empty city-block-long streets remain to remind everyone of the disaster. Most of the survivors are now dead.

Yet, on cloudy nights, the flicker of the burning flares, as their light is reflected off low clouds, is a small reminder of the nights in 1947, when the sky looked like it might actually be an entrance to the gates of hell.

The Texas City Terminal Railway Company, dba The Port of Texas City, has the current regulations:

- #261 NO SMOKING: "No person shall smoke or have in their possession any fire or lighted material upon or near any dock or wharf."
- #262 FIREFIGHTING: "No person shall obstruct or interfere with the free and easy access to, or remove, or in any other manner disturb any fire extinguisher, hose, hydrant, or any other firefighting apparatus upon or near any dock or wharf."

The above regulations are strictly enforced and monitored by the harbormaster and the security division of the Texas City Port Authority.

Editor's Note

W. Michael (Mike) McCrocklin went to his eternal rest in the arms of his Savior on May 22, 2023. He served his Lord for 56 years as an ordained minister and, like his parents, shared his faith at most opportunities throughout his life.

PLEASE REVIEW

You have reached the awkward part of the book where we ask you to leave a review on Amazon, Google, or Goodreads. Whether you loved or hated it, you have made it this far, so please leave a review. Here's the thing: reviews play a big role in determining whether or not someone will read this book. Leaving a review will help us out a lot. If you liked this study, please recommend it to others. Oh, and thanks for reading this book. It means the world to us!

We can't stand typos. If you are like us, you can't either. Typos are like gremlins. No matter how many times this book has been edited, they magically appear. So, if you see a typo we missed, please email Tim at timothyjmulder@gmail.com. Thanks!

More by W. Michael McCrocklin

Jesus of Nazareth: Son of God, Son of Man

Jesus of Nazareth: A Trilogy of Truth

Our Perfect God

Roaming Through Romans

The Doctrines of Grace In the Songs of Israel

The Beginning of God's Beginnings: Genesis Briefly Explained

Mark's Gospel: A Primary Description of Jesus

A Soldier's Lament: Habakkuk: Struggling with Providence

An Encouragement to Reformed Elders

Mysterion: The Mystery of Redemption

John's Gospel: A Short Study

Hebrews: Basic Christology

Neo-Puritanism: Reclaiming Reformation

Jude: A Search for Moral Seriousness

Red River Rout: A Civil War Historic Novel

Bois d'Arc Bowling in the Dark: A Galveston County Lad's Memoirs